# Enjoy The Journey

Creating Wealth and Living the Life You Desire

Jackson Millan- The Wealth Mentor

# Contents

# Testimonials

Jackson Millan - The Wealth Mentor is an International best selling author in 8 countries over 15 categories and has been ranked #1 on Amazon in the US, Australia, Japan and France. Our rankings on Amazon are as follows;

#1 in Kindle Store > Kindle eBooks > Business & Money > Finance (USA) #1 in Kindle Store > Kindle eBooks > Business & Money (USA) #1 in Kindle Store > Kindle eBooks > Business & Money > Personal Finance > Budgeting & Money Management > Money Management (USA) #1 in Kindle Store > Kindle eBooks > Business & Money > Personal Finance > Budgeting & Money Management (USA) #1 in Kindle Store > Kindle eBooks > Business & Money > Personal Finance (USA) #4 in Kindle Store > Kindle eBooks > Nonfiction (USA) #2 in Kindle Store > Books > Business & Finance > Personal Finance (UK) #1 dans Boutique Kindle > Ebooks Kindle > Ebooks en langues étrangères > Ebooks en anglais > Business & Investing > Personal Finance > Budgeting & Money Management (France) #3 en Tienda Kindle > eBooks Kindle > eBooks en idiomas extranjeros > eBooks en inglés > Economics and business (Spain) #1 — Kindle Kindle > Business & Investing > Personal Finance (Japan) #2 — Kindle > Kindle > Business & Investing > Finance (Japan) #4 in Kindle Store > Kindle eBooks > English and Other Languages > eBooks in English > Self-help and personal development (Brazil) #1 in Kindle Store > Kindle eBooks > Business & Investing > Personal Finance > Budgeting & Money Management (Canada) #1 in Kindle Store > Kindle eBooks > Business & Investing > Personal Finance > Money Management (AUS)

'Enjoy The Journey' has achieved an average 5 star review rating. Here's what some of the reviewers have said:

"Loved reading this book! I really enjoyed the practical, "how to approach" in getting my finances in order. It was written in a very relatable way and at times it felt like we were actually having a conversation.. I say relatable because the author showed vulnerability by sharing war stories and really tapping into the mindset or relationship that we have with money.

If you are wanting a practical step by step guide on how to get ahead with your finances , then this book is for you. Great read , thanks Jackson !"

- Ryan Goodfellow

"This book doesn't just give you very handy and easy to follow tools to understand your current financial situation and goals and how to get there but also really delves into understanding your relationship to money, how you can change it for the better and explains the power it can have to help us reach our goals in life. Best of all you can sign up to a portal to download all the tools described in the book and watch short 3 min help videos. I really love this book and it gave me a lot more clarity around why I want to save my money and invest and all the things to consider and making sure I have my plan B in place."

- Nina

"A thought provoking read by an author whose forward thinking concepts will help many to achieve their goals, future financial needs and aspirations. I will recommend this book to colleagues & friends"

- Maureen Terry

"As an entrepreneur and an individual on my own personal journey to financial independence - I actively seek out books to improve my financial literacy.

I found this book a fantastic read, with actionable take-aways and advice that's invaluable for anyone looking to build a life of true financial independence.

The author's writing style was refreshingly conversational, and that really helped simplify some complex ideas."

- Dennis

# Introduction

Money is a fickle beast, and in my experience, I have seen the tremendous impact that it has on the lives of everyone I have ever encountered. I want you to think about the first memorable experience you ever had with money. I want you to close your eyes for a minute, recall all of the smallest details, and get into the mind of your past self.

What do you feel? Was your memory of a positive or a negative experience? Has that experience contributed to shaping your relationship with money today?

I remember my first significant experience with money, when I was around eight years old, which was the catalyst for beginning my wealth journey. For some reason, I still carry this memory, and the feelings of confusion I had harboured until this day, as if it happened yesterday. My nanna Claire gave me a birthday card with $50 in it. As my mum was taking me to the theme parks on the Gold Coast for the first time, I was so excited, as I had never been given money as a gift before. And I was already planning all of the awesome things I would buy when I was there.

"Spend it wisely, Jackson. You are a big boy now, and that's a lot of money, you know!" she said to me with a big smile and a chuckle.

I remember the feeling of responsibility of carrying the money along with all the thoughts going through my head and all the endless possibilities of what I could use it for. Little did I know I was going to be in for a rude awakening.

After a fun-filled day at Sea World, my mum and I went to the gift shop on the way out, and I found a plush toy shark that I fell in love with. I had to have it as soon as I saw it. I picked it up and ran to the counter. With a big grin on my face, I handed over my crisp $50 note that I had in my holographic Billabong wallet. As I waited, I gazed around the gift shop thinking of what else I would buy with my money. But as the woman handed me the bag and the receipt, I quickly realized something was wrong.

"Excuse me. Where is the rest of my change?" I asked her innocently, with only a $10 note remaining in my hand, I was expecting there to be some kind of mistake.

She looked at me blankly, saying, "Well, there isn't any more change, dear, as that toy is forty dollars."

I was speechless and filled with mixed emotions as I walked back to my mum. She immediately noticed the significant difference between my initial excited mood and my now-deflated one.

"What happened, mate? Is everything alright?" she asked, as any concerned mother would.

"Well, I thought the money I had would last longer than it did . . . ," I responded as I pondered over what I had just learned.

Why was this experience so impactful to me? I understood the logic, and I was always decent at math, so I understood that I hadn't been short-changed during the transaction. But still, the thought of having the most money I had ever owned being decimated in a single transaction was shocking to me. This shark toy would act as a metaphor for how money circled everyone I knew as they sank into the depths of the abyss known as financial hardship.

Have you ever had the experience that your money has never quite lasted as long as you expected? Have you been in a situation where you expected to have more money than you did, only to quickly find out at the checkout when you see the decline message on the EFTPOS machine? I know most of us have been there. But have you ever stopped to ask why this happens, and, further, what could be done to prevent it?

My experience has set me on the path to where I am today and has allowed me to help thousands of Australians redefine the relationship they have with money in order to achieve outcomes that they had only dreamed of achieving. This plush shark has served as a symbol for consumerism and the impact this endless cycle of consumerism has on most people's finances leading them into a bottomless pit of debt and financial hardship: a lifetime of receiving decline messages at the checkout, constantly scrambling to keep above water, and spending over thirty years in retirement while relying on the government for support.

There is an unspoken rule in modern society that you shouldn't talk to others about your money. When we are kids, our parents teach us to keep this information private and to share the details of our wealth only with those closest to us. In contrast, with record-high divorce rates being constantly publicized in the media, it seems the conversation of interpersonal relationships is a much easier subject to openly discuss.

Have you ever stopped to ask why these two subjects are treated differently, especially when studies show that over 60 percent of relationship breakdowns are the result of financial issues?

My mission is to challenge the relationship every person in this world has with money. You could refer to me as a wealth relationship counsellor. And my mission is to give every single person on this earth access to the tools needed to sit down face to face with money, dig deep into lifelong financial issues, and make a pact to never fall back into a dysfunctional relationship with money ever again. Additionally, I want to get you talking about your journey and sharing it with those around you. Our life experiences are what ultimately shapes us into who we are. And through sharing our experiences, we can find strength in the similar experiences we share with those around us.

My commitment to you is simple. I want you to confront your journey to date, learn all of the strategies you will ever need to craft your own path, and set out on a mission to obtain everything you have ever desired and more while making a meaningful impact on those around you.

## Sounds too good to be true, right? Wrong.

This book will serve as the only guide you will ever need to achieving a life of abundance and financial freedom, and altering the fate of your loved ones for generations to come. My aim has been to construct a method that will allow you to master the language of money and give you all of the necessary tools to empower those around you, including your partner, children, and friends, to break the cycle once and for all and realize your potential, which is normally reserved for the elite few.

Now, I have something for you naysayers.

I did not come from wealthy beginnings or have a head start provided by my parents. I come from a long chain of working class: my father was a rigger working in the oil and gas industry, and my mother was a hairdresser and aged care worker. Although they worked very hard and did in fact own a number of properties over the course of their lifetimes, they were never wealthy, and they always struggled with money. Both of my parents suffered from accidents and illnesses. These events threw them further into financial hardship due to their lack of emergency funds and adequate insurance coverage. Their wealth journey was an endless uphill battle, and they never managed to get the right advice, guidance, or financial education to help them get ahead.

Why should you listen to me?

Well, I have spent the last ten years crafting my proprietary "Values Based Advice" system, which has allowed me to work with over one thousand clients, manage over $500 million in investment assets, and help my clients accumulate over $1 billion in combined wealth. As part of this, I have been lucky enough to be recognized as Financial Adviser of the Year, and my businesses have won a number of other national industry awards. I have owned a number of businesses and trained over thirty advisers. I am now on a mission to change the world of wealth education and advice to ensure that all people have access to the right resources to improve their financial situation and work toward financial freedom. Not bad for a twenty-eight-year-old, huh?

So why am I doing this? Well, we all know that there isn't any money in books anymore, so I am definitely not doing this to get rich. It is time to shift control back into the hands of the people and away from the financial institutions. I aim to achieve this through education, empowerment, and the right advice to help get you where you want to go.

Are you ready to get started?

## Legal Disclaimer

Every effort has been made to offer the most current, correct and clearly expressed information possible within this site. Nonetheless, inadvertent errors can occur and applicable laws, rules and regulations may change.

The information contained in this site is general and is not intended to serve as advice. No warranty is given in relation to the accuracy or reliability of any information. Users should not act or fail to act on the basis of information contained herein. Users are encouraged to contact The Wealth Mentor, an entity of Aureus Financial, a representative of Dover Financial Advisers professional advisers for advice concerning specific matters before making any decision.

Aureus Wealth Advisers Pty Ltd (CAR 1259968) and Jackson Millan (AR 344212) are Authorised Representatives of Dover Financial Advisers Pty Ltd ACN 112 139 321 and AFSL 307248.

# About the Author

*Jackson Millan started his advice career at nineteen and has always been an ambitious individual striving to outperform. His goal has always been to remove the complication that most associate with managing their finances and create simple and sustainable strategies that his clients understand and embrace to work toward their own idea of financial freedom.*

*Working with the largest financial institutions in Australia, Jackson quickly started to realize that the industry as a whole does little to serve its clients and help them make meaningful change in their lives. This led to Jackson founding The Wealth Mentor, a thought-leadership initiative helping educate and empower the masses to take control of their financial future. Jackson is also the cofounder of Aureus Financial, a revolutionary financial services and wealth coaching business focused on giving people access to a team of experts to support their wealth journey in pursuit of their goals.*

*As the founder of the "Values Based Advice" system, Jackson and his team aim to provide wealth solutions to everyone ranging from books, e-learning courses, wealth coaching, and bespoke advice. He believes that everyone deserves to have access to the tools required to work toward financial freedom and aims to act as the catalyst for change in a stale industry that only aims to serve itself.*

*Jackson has received the national award Adviser of the Year. His businesses have been named Branch of the Year, Wealth Business of the Year, Multiservice Business of the Year, and Customer Service Business of the Year finalist.*

Make sure you sign up to the book portal for the most optimal reading experience. We have developed a series of videos, cheat sheets and activities that will help you apply the knowledge, take action and set yourself on the right path for success. Most books only give you one piece of the puzzle and you leave not knowing what to do next so we have simplified every module of the book into easy to implement action plans to ensure you break the cycle and kick some serious goals!

### JOIN NOW FOR FREE AT
book.wealth-mentor.com.au

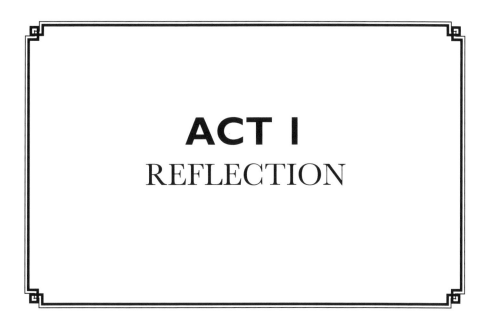

# ACT I
## REFLECTION

# CHAPTER I

# What Is Holding You Back?

You have purchased or have been given this book for a reason. I'm sorry to be the bearer of bad news, but that reason is likely because you haven't hit the jackpot yet—reality hits you hard, mate! But that isn't a bad thing. And something has inspired you, or someone who cares for you has given you this book, to help you reach your fullest potential. Honestly, how many people do you know who have truly reached their potential in life? How many people do you know who have paid off their homes, have built substantial wealth, and will be able to supplement their lifestyles entirely from passive income for the rest of their lives? Who do you know who has mastered the game of life and is in a position to leave a memorable legacy for generations to come? I know from firsthand experience that these people are few and far between.

My father, Mario Millan, immigrated to Australia from Chile when he was twenty-one years old. I don't know much about why he chose Australia, but I know that he came here to make the most of his life, and he worked his ass off until the day he died. I remember my father telling me a story of when he arrived and how he found a job as a labourer in the coke works at Corrimal in Wollongong which produced fuel for the refinery at the steel works. He turned up to his first day in acid wash jeans, a John Travolta shirt, a leather jacket, and cowboy boots (the '70s, right?). By the end of his first day, he left the place covered head to toe in black soot with his clothes completely tattered and ruined.

I guess this beginning isn't too different from that of most of this country's first-generation immigrants, who had to endure great hardship to set themselves up. Unlike many of these hard-working immigrants, my father never caught a break to build any real wealth in this land of opportunity. I remember all the stories he used to tell me about how close he came to making it big-time through missed opportunities in property, business, and other lucrative ventures that never quite seemed to work out. As such, he was caught in the struggle of constantly having to work to live. At the age of sixty-six, he died of pancreatic cancer without ever being able to experience what it was like to be free of financial burden. Until the day he died, he carried the heavy weight of the mess he knew he would leave behind.

My father was a tough man, and I can only remember seeing him cry three times (all caused by me, of course). I vividly remember the moment I held his cold hands as he lay there in his hospital bed, fighting to put on a strong face as he tried to talk to me through his tears.

"I am sorry for not being able to do more. . . I am sorry for leaving all of my mistakes behind for you to carry on your own," he said as he stared into my eyes, knowing that he had run out of time.

"I just wish I had more time . . . more time to do things differently . . ."

He passed away a few days later. As of writing this book, I am still working to finalize his estate and the complexities of his financial situation, which involved the significant amount of debt he accumulated through trying to fight his illness for seven years.

This subject hits home for me and I am sure for many of you reading this, as most of us have probably found ourselves hoping for more time and pleading for an opportunity to do things differently. For years I saw my father as an unlucky man who could have lived an amazing life filled with financial abundance if only the dice were rolled differently. From my experience, this is how most of us view the world. We expect that the game called life will play us whatever cards we're dealt and that we just have to make the most of them. Unfortunately, this mentality pushes us into being victims of circumstance and presupposes that we are unable to alter our financial fate or the fate of those around us.

That is 100 percent not true!

My father was a great man, a smart man, and my idol, and he taught me how to be who I am today. He showed me what it meant to be headstrong and how to work hard for what I want. What my father was never able to teach me—and for that matter, what his father was never able to teach him—was how to understand the language of money and make it work for me. He always tried his best to teach me about money. He tried to get me to save for what he referred to as a rainy day. He tried to instil values in me that I should always save 20 percent of everything I earned—a great lesson in theory, but for some reason it never resonated with me (or with him, for that matter, as he never practiced what he preached).

What was the flaw in his approach to money that prevented him from achieving the financial success he tried to teach me? Why was it that his lessons never inspired me to take action?

The missing link was that he treated money and wealth as if they were the destination. This is a common theme among most people and a huge flaw in their plan to achieve financial freedom.

Money is not the destination. It is the vehicle that allows us to reach the destination that we desire.

You may ask, But Jackson, what's the difference?

Let's paint a picture for you to put it all in perspective. I will ask you a few questions.

Before I do, clear your mind, and take these questions at face value without your logical brain asking the question "What do you mean by that?" Look straight ahead, and then move your eyes up to the top right of your vision and stare in that direction, pondering the questions one at a time until you have a clear picture of what comes to mind.

1    What is fundamentally important to you? What do you need every day to feel safe and secure?

2    Assuming you have that and you feel content with all of your fundamental needs, what then becomes your goals, dreams, or aspirations?

3    What is the significance to you of achieving those goals, dreams, or aspirations?

Take the time to ask these questions to yourself until you can no longer think of what else you want and are completely content with everything that has come up.

Now ask yourself, honestly, were any of your desires to have money itself, or was it material things, experiences, or objectives that you truly desire?

Of course, most, if not all, of these things require money to become a reality for you. However, this proves that money is only the vehicle to get you where you want to go. We will dive into this exercise in more detail later. I will explain how it works and how to use visualization as a powerful method to create a million-dollar mindset.

Now back to the story of my old man. What exactly did he do wrong that ultimately determined his financial destiny?

•    He always assumed his earned income would make him rich. He earned on average $150,000–$200,000 per annum but still never ended up being wealthy.

- He used credit as a buffer against emergencies, which spiralled out of control.

- He was never able to define what he wanted financially and, in turn, how he planned to get to his destination.

- He was unable to defer the gratification of short-term financial decisions for increased gratification in the future.

- He tried to do everything himself and never relied on the advice of experts to get things done.

Why am I telling you this?

I promised my father a number of things during his last days. Those things are

1. I am going to break the cycle of just getting by financially and create a meaningful change for myself and all future generations to come,

2. I am going to do everything in my power to change the world through wealth education and awareness, and

3. I will do everything I can to make him proud of the man I have grown to become.

I want to break the cycle, and I want to challenge each of you to come to terms with your own finances and the demons that have plagued you for years (and maybe even your family for generations). I am a huge believer in the saying "In order to know where you are going, you need to know where you have come from." So now is time to come to terms with your story and share it openly, regardless of how painful that reality may be.

With this, I want you to make a promise to yourself right now that you are going to commit 100 percent to altering the course of your future, even if only by 1 percent. This promise is going to be a binding contract to hold yourself accountable for getting to your final destination.

You have nothing to be ashamed of. It is never too late. There is nowhere you can't come back from, no matter how far astray you feel you are from your final destination. Now, are you ready to take control of your own financial future and be the author of your own wealth journey?

Why aren't you one of these people who is able to live a life of complete abundance? No, it's not because you haven't won the lottery yet. In actual fact, most lottery winners end up in a worse financial position than they were in when they started. After reading this book and learning the simple formula for constructing your roadmap to financial freedom, you will know exactly what to do with every dollar. On the off chance you do win the lottery, you will avoid falling into the traps that most of the winners before you have found themselves in.

## Eleven Reasons Why You Aren't Wealthy Yet:

1. You spend first and save later and have no set amount of surplus.

2. You don't know what you need to do each day to work toward your goals.

3. You believe you lack the time to manage your money better.

4. You weren't ever taught how to manage your money.

5. You are afraid of shares or growth assets due to the fear of losing money.

6. You believe in waiting for the best opportunity to present itself before investing.

7. You have a mountain of debt and have no idea how to tackle it.

8. You don't earn enough money to get ahead.

9. You believe you have missed the boat to get into the property market.

10. You don't want to sacrifice your lifestyle to plan for the future.

11. You believe you don't have enough time left to plan.

What is the common theme among all of the above? Have you ever found the voice in your head telling yourself these excuses? Well, this is how we justify our reality and allow ourselves to come to terms with the status quo. What you need to know is that this isn't acceptable and that an excuse is the most expensive mistake you will ever make in your life.

Our mind is an amazing and efficient machine that contains thousands of defence mechanisms to keep us safe from harm. We develop these reflexes over the course of our lives, and these reflexes guide us through life using the path of least resistance. I always use the saying "Life always tends to get in the way," and it stands true in this instance. As we live our day-to-day life, our subconscious guides us through everything we are used to doing automatically with almost no effort at all.

Can you recall the first time you drove a car and how many thoughts were going through your head? You were thinking of the acceleration, the mirrors, the indicators. You were steering and trying to be mindful of all of the things going on around you. As you went from being unconsciously incompetent prior to driving, you now consciously came to terms with everything you didn't know about operating a vehicle.

Now think of a route you drive all of the time, whether it be the commute to work or your favourite place to drive on the weekend. Have you ever found yourself jumping in the car, drifting off into thought, and arriving at your destination without any recollection of how you actually got there? This is exactly what you do with your money, and you are now unconsciously incompetent about how you manage your wealth.

What do we need to do about that? We can either keep drifting off into space and come to terms with the reality of where we ultimately end up when we reach our destination, or we can grab hold of the wheel, take control, and change our course for the greater good. To put this in perspective, I am going to take you on a journey.

Clear your mind and immerse yourself in the following story. I want you to take the driver's seat and create a version of yourself that is able to connect with all of the details and feelings that come up along the way. This may feel a little strange. Please trust the process, trust yourself, and know that everything will be OK.

You are walking down a highway at sunset, and there are no cars or other people anywhere in sight. There is a light breeze, and the sun is setting over the horizon in front of you. As you walk, you have no real destination in mind, but you are compelled to keep walking, as you know this is what you are supposed to do. You feel your heart beating rapidly, and your breath is heavy as you continue to walk. You are tired, and your eyelids are heavy, but you push on, as this is what your mind tells you. "I am heading in the right direction."

You come across a motorcycle on the side of the road with the keys in the ignition. You have never ridden before, but you have always wanted to learn. Your mind tells you that you shouldn't risk it, but your heart tells you to give it a try. But the bike isn't yours, and the owner isn't anywhere in sight. There is a note taped to the side of the tank. You pull it off to read it. It says,

"I have left this here for you, as I have used it to get to where I need to go. Good luck on your journey."

You already know how to walk. You have done it for years and years, and walking has never failed you. It hasn't gotten you anywhere fast. But why would you want to get anywhere in a hurry anyway? You know motorcycles are dangerous. With no one to teach you how to ride it, there is a big chance you may fail and hurt yourself. But it's getting dark, and you need to get somewhere safe before night falls.

What do you choose to do? Where does your choice take you? How does your choice make you feel? What could have happened if you chose differently?

When was the last time you made an active decision to determine the path you would take in your life? Can you recall the last time you decided that something needed to change and that you were going to do all in your power to change the reality of your situation? More often than not, these forks in the road are few and far between because we tend to never take the time to step back from the situation and assess what choices we have.

Now come to terms with your reality. You aren't rich yet, and this reality is 100 percent your choice. You are either going to keep walking down the lonely highway as the darkness falls over you or you are going to take a leap of faith, jump on that motorcycle, turn the key, and allow yourself to consciously accept your incompetence while you learn how to ride. You might fall along the way. You might get a flat tyre or run out of fuel. But you know deep down that this decision will get you where you want to go faster if you endure the journey in pursuit of your final destination. You know this because you know that something needs to change.

In the famous words of Warren Buffett, "We pay a big price for certainty." It is a matter of our working out how much risk we are prepared to take in order to get to our destination.

CHAPTER 2

# Applying For Your License: Learning The Language of Money

Let's get one thing straight: money is a fickle beast, and we spend a lot of our life trying to understand it, master it, and make it work for us. But with more than 2.9 million, or approximately 13 percent, of all Australians living below the poverty line, there are strong signs to show that a lot of us have absolutely no idea what we are doing when it comes to wealth. Furthermore, less than 10 percent of our population is actively seeking financial advice. Many of these 2.4 million people are unhappy with the service they receive. Honestly, I don't blame them, because the system is broken! We will get more into this later on.

An MLC study in 2016 showed the scary fact that three out of five Australians no longer thought that having $1,000,000 meant one was rich and that close to 50 percent of Australians thought that they needed more than $150,000 a year to live "comfortably." The statistic that really hit home for me was that 69 percent of all surveyed were feeling the pain of keeping up with their living expenses on a week-to-week basis and needed to live pay check to pay check. Why do so many of us struggle with money and get caught in this vicious cycle of survival?

Well, the answer is pretty simple to understand when you think about it.

Let's change up the scenario a little. The world has gone to shit. All governments have been dissolved. Money no longer has value. All of the assets you owned, such as cash, shares, and property, are pretty much worthless. The currency of choice is anything that you can eat or that will keep you alive. Barter is how you get what you need to keep on keeping on.

That sounds pretty grim, right?

In this time, your decisions around how you accumulate, ration, and protect your resources is ultimately going to determine your fate and that of your family, who you are responsible for protecting and keeping safe and healthy as you all battle to survive.

With this fresh perspective on life, what would you do differently? Would you consume all of your resources recklessly and just expect things to work themselves out? Would you work hard to barter for a bag of rice and eat it all on the first day, knowing that you might have to wait a long time before you got the next bag? If you knew you needed to accumulate building materials over a long period of time in order to make a long-lasting shelter for your family, no matter how long it took, would you choose to stockpile wood, nails, tools, and other necessary items with the future goal of having safety and security? Or would you just choose to let life guide you and hope for the best?

Perspective is everything. Unfortunately, these life-and-death circumstances don't exist for most of us. We tend to always want more than what we have. But what we have always gives us enough security to not have the sense of urgency that would exist in a post-apocalyptic world. This concept is referred to as *deferred gratification*. For most of us, our life consists of small and steady amounts of gratification from our day-to-day decisions, such as buying that $5 goji berry chai latte in the morning, taking an Uber home instead of getting on the train, or those purchasing new shoes that were on sale that you might only wear a few times before they sit in the closet collecting dust. These small gratifying decisions give us that instant pleasure or release of endorphins that helps us get through the mundanity of everyday life.

Don't get me wrong. I am guilty of doing these very things myself. I have a passion for vintage motorbikes, and I spend plenty of money keeping my fifty-year-old Harley Davidson on the road. This isn't about deferring all gratification. This is about allocating enough resources for the short, medium, and long term by using rational thought to keep us on track to make informed and educated decisions around our wealth.

I don't want to go all propeller-hat geek mode on you, but I need you to understand the science behind what is actually going on in that mind of yours. We need to take a moment to step back and reflect on what the hell is going on up there so that we can pull ourselves up the next time we fall off the wagon. We need to go from unconsciously incompetent to consciously incompetent if we want to take the first step toward becoming money masters!

## Mmm, Marshmallows

As children we are programmed to do what is necessary to get what we want. Our parents constantly remind us that if we want something, we need to ask for it or work for it. In the 1960s, this was proven through a study at Stanford University that attempted to understand strategies that preschool kids used to resist temptation. The study has been recreated in a YouTube video called "The Marshmallow Test," which is very cute and definitely worth checking out. Basically, four-year-old kids were given a marshmallow and advised that they could immediately eat the marshmallow if they wanted. But if they waited just fifteen minutes without eating the marshmallow, the facilitator would give them a second marshmallow.

Having been a four-year-old child, you can imagine the physical pain they would feel having to wait fifteen minutes for anything they really wanted. Reflect on yourself as a child. Do you think you could have waited fifteen minutes, or would you have stuffed that marshmallow into your mouth as quickly as possible? I know that I would have gobbled that marshmallow as soon as the facilitator left the room!

The results of the study and every replication of the study since have shown that two out of three kids were unable to defer gratification. At some point during the fifteen minutes, they gave into temptation and ate the marshmallow. One out of three kids were able to stay occupied. They smelled the marshmallow, played with it, and battled through temptation just so that they could get their second marshmallow at the end of the fifteen minutes.

The most interesting part of the study is when the kids were interviewed years later as teenagers and adults. The results were pretty scary. The kids who were able to defer gratification were good students, had well-thought-out plans for their future, and were all around happy and successful at school and in their working lives. The kids who were unable to resist temptation had mostly poor grades, had dropped out of school, had no real direction in life, and were overall unhappy with what they had achieved so far.

The study was reinforced by the cognitive-affective processing system theory, which basically describes the process of how a person uses regulating strategies to overcome temptation by using *hot* or *cool* strategies. Hot strategies involve the emotional, impulsive, and automatic reactions that were used by the two out of three kids that couldn't wait. Cool strategies involve distraction and changing the perception of the tempting stimulus to make it seem less appealing. These were used by the one out of three kids that sang songs, played games, or paced the room to stay distracted while waiting.

This study is fantastic because it makes us aware of the power of deferring gratification. However, all of this theory provides no practical tools that we can use to alter our fate. I don't believe that we are born as either the kid who scoffs the marshmallow or the one who patiently waits by using cool strategies to pass the time in order to reap the rewards of sacrifice. There are many shades of grey depending on the situation, our life experience, and how much we want to achieve the end outcome. As such, I am going to teach you one of the most powerful lessons you will ever learn. This will be the first weapon in your arsenal to achieve financial freedom.

Here is a very simple question for you. Ponder on it for as long as you can, asking yourself the question over and over until you have complete clarity.

What do you want?

Take your time here. What do *you* want?

Got it? Great. Paint a vivid picture in your mind of exactly what that thing is, down to the smallest details, as if it were right in front of you. Take note of all of the colours, smells, sensations, and feelings you experience.

How do you feel when you are in this moment, visualizing what you want?

Remove all of the irrelevant details that come up along the way. Remove all of the distractions around you and all of the things that might get in the way of your getting what you want.

- What will have this do for you?
- How will you know when you have it?
- When, where, and with whom do you want it?
- Once you have it, what might you lose that you value?

This exercise is how we can change ourselves from the two-thirds of kids to the one-third of kids and get all of the marshmallows we want in the world. Through visualization and attaching our current state to our desired future state, we are able to create a conscious connection among what we want, the feelings we will experience when we get there, and the value of the sacrifice we will make in order to get there.

With these tools, I want you to map out what you want. Identify what areas of wealth and future planning need your immediate attention. Remember, we only want to learn the language that is relevant to us. One of my protégés was always one for analogies. One of my favourites was as follows:

Imagine you are going to book a trip. You head into the travel agency. "So, should I take a plane, a bus, a train, or a ferry?" you ask. "I've heard the seaside is really nice this time of year."

What is the first thing they will ask you?

"Well, where is it that you want to go?"

The same concept stands true here. Let's work on what you want so that we can work out which gaps you need to fill to help you get there. We will go into this further in the next chapter.

# CHAPTER 3

# Defining the Destination: What Do You Really Want?

When was the last time you went on a journey? Was it a weekend getaway or an overseas trip? Did you just decide to go spontaneously, or did you plan where you wanted to go for months in advance to ensure that everything was arranged and booked prior to your departure?

For many of us, the thought of just waking up one morning and leaving in pursuit of a destination unknown with nothing but the bag on our back and the money in our wallet is a fantasy. But very few of us ever do this. Why? Well, because the fear of the unknown and the lack of a plan to follow tends to scare most of us. We never want to end up stranded in the middle of nowhere with no money, no place to stay, and no food.

So why don't you have a plan for what you want to achieve between now and the rest of your life? This isn't just about money. This is about everything you want to achieve in your life, whether that be related to career, self, family, wealth, lifestyle, or community. When was the last time you sat down to work out *exactly* what you wanted out of your life and by when you wanted to achieve these goals?

For most of us, there are some fundamental reasons why we don't do this. The simple reason for this is that most of us aren't taught how to be ambitious or taught to reach for the stars. We are constantly given the message that we just need to get good grades at school, go to university, get a good job, work hard, and everything will work itself out. But does it really?

As a kid, I had amazing parents that were always supportive of what I wanted to do with my life, but they never held me accountable for seeing things through to the end. I was always an adventurous kid. I tried every hobby under the sun, including soccer, football, hockey, tae kwon do, kung fu, karate, piano, guitar, cadets—the list goes on. I was always good at starting something, but for whatever reason, I always managed to find an excuse not to continue with whatever I was doing.

Sound familiar?

This was the earliest sign of my self-sabotage. Through years of starting and quitting my interests, I developed a habit of never seeing things through. This ultimately manifested into me becoming frustrated with school and dropping out in year eleven to get a job. My parents were furious with me. They had always told me that to be successful in life, I needed to always get good grades, apply myself, and go to university. Otherwise, I would never be successful. For whatever reason, this never resonated with me, and I always did the bare minimum at school and received average report cards, with teachers constantly saying the same thing,

"Jackson is a bright kid but is easily distracted and needs to apply himself if he wants to reach his potential."

This was the story of my life as a kid, and I always expected that things would work themselves out. From the youngest age I can remember, I always wanted to be a veterinarian. I never deviated from this for my entire childhood until I reached year nine, when this dream was shattered for me. I never really understood what I needed to do in order to become a vet. Because of my lack of direction and my lack of commitment to school work, a teacher advised me that I needed an extremely high score to get into veterinary science in university and that there was only a limited amount of positions within the course each year. The teacher said that it would be extremely unlikely for me to get in, even if I applied myself.

Well shit, there goes that idea!

With my teenage mentality, I just gave up, did even less at school, and got into trouble. Ultimately, I got to year eleven and decided school wasn't of any value to me. I went to see the principal to drop out along with a friend of mine who wanted to do the same. My friend was one of the smartest guys I knew and was always in the highest classes in math, science, and English. I thought he would end up getting amazing grades and being really successful in a white-collar job that paid well.

When we sat down in the principal's office, he asked us for our best excuse before allowing us to go to our parents to get signed off for dropping out of school. We both looked at each other and sat silently for a minute while we shrugged our shoulders and tried to think of an intelligent answer.

"Well, sir, we feel that we are wasting our time here when we could be out making real money," I said, with a confident teenage smile.

"Hmm, is that right? So where exactly are you going to be making this real money?" he asked in response.

We didn't have a good answer for that and sat there blankly.

"The condition for you to leave is that you need to go meet with the careers counsellor, so he can give you some good options to pursue once you leave. Once you speak with him, come back to me, and we will discuss it further."

Fantastic! This seemed like the best possible outcome. Off we went to see the career adviser, who was a funny little man, and he sat down with us in his office.

"So, boys, you want to get out into the real world, hey? So, what exactly do you want to do for work?"

Once again, we looked at each other blankly and pondered for a moment.

"Well, we just want to make lots of money . . ."

He stared back at us, raising an eyebrow before responding.

"You realize that most jobs that pay well need you to go to university, right?"

"Yeah, but there must be jobs that pay well that don't require us to stay in this place, sir," my friend said, laughing.

The adviser stopped for a second to think. An idea suddenly hit him.

"So, there's this machine, right? It's an X-ray machine that a guy will use to check concrete for cancer, and he makes a fair bit of money from that." He said this convincingly as if he had come up with the best idea in the world.

"Concrete cancer? Are you serious, sir?" I asked, checking if he was joking.

He was dead serious. My friend and I looked at each other, stood up, and left. We dropped out a few days later and went out to get jobs.

It's pretty safe to say I never ended up buying the machine or going into the concrete cancer industry.

Why am I telling you this story? Like most kids, I lacked the tools needed to create a plan toward what I wanted to achieve, and I lacked the support needed to make the right decisions to get where I wanted to go. I was the two out of three marshmallow kids who couldn't defer the short-term gratification of wasting time and playing around in order to achieve my goals. I was expecting that everything would work itself out and that I would end up where I wanted to go with little effort at all. Furthermore, the environment I grew up in lacked the fundamental knowledge I needed to be empowered to choose a path in life that didn't necessarily require attending university, achieving straight As in every class, or becoming the valedictorian of my school.

My experience taught me a number of important lessons:

1.  Our parents tend to teach us based on their experiences and try to protect us from the mistakes they made, assuming we will suffer the same fate.

2.  The education system aims to provide the same structure for all kids, assuming all learn and develop in the same way. Would you judge a fish by its ability to climb a tree?

3.  Our individual strengths and weaknesses are not identified and leveraged to reach our fullest potential.

4.  We lack the resources to use these strengths and weaknesses to develop an individual plan that gets us where we want to go and nurtures us to achieve our goals.

5.  Our government has allowed corporations into the classroom to teach our kids about money, which inevitably traps them in a vicious cycle of consumerism and bad debt.

6.  We all need a plan, no matter how old we are, what we have achieved, or where we want to go.

So, let's get back to the journey. Let's work out where exactly we want to go. Then we will work together to make a plan that will become a living, breathing document that you will carry with you and update for the rest of your life.

Remember, poor planning leads to piss-poor performance!

I want you to go back to your childhood and remember what you wanted more than anything when you were a child. There should be a stand-out memory of one thing you really wanted, obsessed over, never stopped talking about, and always bugged your parents for. Was it a toy? Was it something else that was special to you?

# CHAPTER 4

# Preparing For The Journey: The Million-Dollar Mindset

One of my mentors, Barry Magliarditi, taught me one of the most profound lessons I have ever learned, and it is so simple that it seems crazy when you think of it. Barry taught me that the difficult situations we learn to survive turn into the situations our survival depends upon.

What the hell does that mean, Jackson?

Have you found yourself asking why you always end up in similar precarious situations or why certain events keep happening to you no matter how you try to prevent them? Do you believe this is just sheer coincidence, or is it something deeper than that?

I am going to geek out on you again. We are going to talk about our brains for a minute. Our brain consists of three parts: The R complex, or the lizard brain; the limbic system; and the neocortex. Each part of the brain plays a very different role. This unique combination is what makes us human.

Our R complex, or lizard brain, is where our basic survival instincts—such as hunger, temperature control, and fight-or-flight reactions—come from. This part of our brain is something that has had millions of years of hard-coded reflex and survival instinct built in. Our limbic brain is our emotional brain and controls our feelings, mood, memory, hormone control, and, most importantly, our decision-making ability. Finally, our neocortex is our thinking brain and is where all complex planning, social interaction, and strategy development comes from.

Now, why is knowing this so important?

We need to understand that the parts of our brain have developed at different times and that our logical brain, which we use consciously every day, and even our emotional brain have very little capacity to communicate with our lizard brain, which controls the reflexes that keep us alive. With this, we need to understand that our lizard brain learns to adapt to situations to keep us alive. With this adaptation, it learns that if it was able to survive a situation once, it will be able to survive it again.

Let's expand on this concept.

You are stranded on a deserted island, and you have been trying to survive for over a week. The weather is unpredictable, and storms happen frequently. You have little shelter to keep you dry and warm. You have run out of food. With no other food source readily available, you are likely to perish if you stay on the island. Although you are tired and have little energy, you are not willing to accept this fate, so you decide to find a way to get off the island.

What do you do?

Do you build a raft? Do you try to make some kind of signal, hoping someone will see it? Why are these the things we instantly think of when visualizing this scenario? Well, these are the kinds of solutions we have seen in movies, TV shows, and so on. We tend to learn survival from either firsthand experience or through observing those around us and how they themselves have learned to survive. Given this is the path of least resistance, our lizard brain has created a synapsis that immediately makes us recall these solutions for survival when we find ourselves in the same situation.

That's a good thing, right? Let's look at this in a different context that might hit home for you as it certainly does for me.

You are a child growing up and learning the ropes of life. Your parents are hard workers. They do their best to provide for you and the family, and they try their best to teach you the values of hard work and dedication. Times are tough. Although you don't go without the necessities, there isn't quite enough for your parents to give you the life they wanted, for them to enjoy as much time as they would like with the family, or for them to have the freedom to go away regularly by themselves to enjoy quality time without the stress of everyday life. Even as this situation shifts, and more money starts to come in, the one commodity that they never have enough of is time, and the freedom they strived for always seems out of reach.

You are an adult now, and you are appreciative for the opportunities and sacrifices your parents made for you. It's your responsibility to take control of your life. Although you have ambitions to do things differently, make more money, and have more time, you are stuck in the same cycle. As soon as you start to make some progress toward the things you want, something always seems to get in the way, and you end up back where you started. You don't go without anything, but progress is slow and takes a lot of hard work for little reward.

Sound familiar? Why?

The difficult situations we learn to survive turn into the situations our survival depends upon.

Our lizard brain has observed the hard work and dedication of the previous generations. It has seen our parents and those around us working hard to survive and struggling to get ahead. It has seen these generations of people learn to adapt to the difficult experiences they found themselves in. Because of this, most of us follow the lead of our lizard brain and do the same as others have done, resulting in an endless cycle of living pay check to pay check and never having quite enough time, money, or both to do what we really want. When our logical brain has had enough, we tell ourselves we have had enough and try and to break out of this pattern.

For most of us, this never happens. And no matter how hard we try, we end up back in a similar situation and accept this as our fate.

Think about the lives your parents lived. Think about the lives of those around you. Think about the life you live right now. Are you 100 percent satisfied with your reality and the reality of those around you, or do you want more than what you experience right now?

If you can honestly tell yourself you are content with where you are, then it is probably best to gift this book to someone else. On the other hand, if you want to better yourself, make more money, have more time, and give more to those around you, then we need to break you out from this cycle that your lizard brain has you caught in.

As a child, I never got the chance to experience a normal family where my mum and dad were both under the same roof, because they separated when I was only a few months old. In reflection, I was lucky because I am sure being old enough to remember my parents splitting up would be a traumatic experience. My parents were always very honest with me, and this honesty has played a vital role in shaping me into the person I am today. I vividly remember when my mother told me why she separated from my father. I remember the words my mum told me. To spare you the graphic details, I've summarized it as follows:

"Your father is a great dad, but he made a terrible husband."

The story my mum told me was raw, violent, and for some reason, it was quite surreal to me at the time. I never judged my father for what he did. But now that he is gone and with what I know, I see that the way he learned to survive was to find his way into battle and then use brute force to find his way out.

My dad was from a different time and grew up in a country that required him to fight to survive. Being the youngest of seven kids in a family that never had much, we had to learn how to be resilient and battle to get what he wanted. Every story my father told me was a story of violence. I remember his telling me that he saw his friend stabbed to death when he was only five years old—the sheer thought of this makes my skin crawl. Having learned to survive by fighting, my dad learned to solve his problems with his fists. I have lost count of the times I saw him lose his temper in a fit of rage that ended in a brawl in the supermarket, the bus, or the sidewalk.

So what effect did all of this have on me?

All throughout school, I was one of the smallest in my grade. As I was an easy target, I always attracted the attention of the school bullies. Each afternoon when my dad would come pick me up from school, I would run up to him and tell him what had happened. His immediate response would be to say,

"Are you going to put up with this shit? As soon as you see that kid again, you are going to punch him straight in the head, no questions asked!"

On more than one occasion, I saw that kid on the way home from school while my father and I rode our bicycles. My dad would look at me and raise his eyebrows as if to say, "Go get him." I was quick to act, and this resulted in more fights than I can keep count of.

I was never a good fighter, and I have lost more fights than I have won. But I found myself in this vicious cycle of violence, which spanned the course of my life up until I was around twenty-one. I remember thinking to myself as I grew older, "I know there is going to be a fight tonight." As if they were gospel, my predictions seemed to always come true.

Was this just a coincidence? Had I somehow developed a sixth sense for violence? Or had the situations I learned to survive become the situations my survival depended upon?

## Survival

I was around twenty-one years old, and it was the night before Mother's Day. I told my mom that I was going out to the city with my friends and that I would be home early so that I could take her out for breakfast the next day. As I went to leave the house, she said to me, with concerned gaze,

"Be safe tonight, and don't get into any trouble, Jack."

"Sure thing, mum" I responded without a second thought as I walked out the door.

A friend of mine picked me up. We went to a bar in the Inner West of Sydney for a hip-hop gig that a friend had put on. We had a few drinks and caught up with our group of friends, and the night went off without a hitch. A normal night out in Sydney, as many of you may know, tends to involve some kind of violence. But this night seemed to be different for a change. Our designated driver was supposed to drive us all home, because we all knew our mums would be livid if we got home in the early hours of the morning and slept through Mother's Day, which I am sure we had all done before as stupid teenagers.

As the crowd started to leave and the bar got ready to close, I looked around for my friend who was driving. He was nowhere to be seen. He was notoriously unreliable, and it looked like he had left without me— probably not the first time or the last time.

Shit. How am I going to get home?

It was around 1:00 a.m. I knew the regular bus and train services had stopped, so I started walking up Parramatta Road toward Central station to catch the Nightrider bus home. The Night Rider bus was appropriately dubbed "the Fight Rider," as it was never a good idea to contain a bunch of drunk people into close quarters. The bus rides always ended up in someone fighting at some point on the journey home.

I bet my bottom dollar something is going to happen to me on that bus!

As I walked toward Broadway Shopping Centre with my headphones in my ears, a guy with a hoodie pulled over his head walked in the opposite direction toward me. The guy was walking very close to my path, and I could see from my peripheral vision that he was looking for a fight. Anyone who knows Sydney after midnight knows that it is always best to look straight ahead in these situations and avoid eye contact. As he walked closer to me, he shoved me with his shoulder. I did my best to roll my body to deflect the blow, and I kept my gaze facing forward. I knew that as soon as I looked back, the situation would erupt.

Phew! It seemed as though the crisis was averted, and I kept walking toward the station. Ahead of me was a glass bus station. Above that was a street lamp that kept it illuminated. The light above the glass turned the glass surface into somewhat of a mirror. As I approached the station, I saw the guy charging at me at full running pace. With sheer good luck and timing, I sidestepped him. Fuelled by reflex, I grabbed the back of his hoodie with his momentum and threw him headfirst into this glass shelter, which shattered into thousands of pieces around him.

As he lay there covered in glass with no sign of life, I ran as fast as I could down George Street until I couldn't run anymore. I called my mum as I had absolutely no idea what to do. I was in complete shock from the situation, which had escalated so quickly from nothing to a potentially life-changing event.

"What's wrong, Jack? Where the hell are you?" Mum yelled, concerned that I wasn't home yet.

"Mum, I think I have just killed a guy who tried to attack me!" I responded in a shaken, quivering voice.

Mum immediately erupted into tears.

"Get in a taxi, and get home now! We will deal with this when you get here."

I got home and told mum everything that had happened. We sat up until the sun rose, watching the news to see if anything had been reported. As we sat there quietly, hours seemed like days, as we knew that whatever we saw could potentially change the course of the rest of our lives.

As we watched the morning news report, I remember the exact words my mother told me that would act as the crossroad that led me to where I am today.

"Jack, every time you leave the house, I worry that I will get a call with two outcomes—that you are either dead or in jail."

As she looked at me, I saw the same way she looked at my father. In this moment, I knew that my life needed to change. Would I accept the reality I had created through the experiences I learned to survive, or would I make a conscious choice to change the way I dealt with the experiences my survival depended upon?

You need to understand that reshaping these survival instincts is extremely difficult, and it requires you to come to terms with potentially generations of baggage that your ancestors have used to survive. You need to come to terms with these fundamental beliefs and be willing to define and adopt new beliefs that will act as your guiding forces for the rest of your natural life along with the lives of generations to come. You need to be willing to believe that you can change your course, which has been set by all of those who came before you, to be your own person and create your own path of your own choosing.

How do you do this?

You need to understand the mindset you currently hold and how you use this to make every decision in your life. You need to identify the roadblocks you currently have in that brain of yours and how they are stopping you from pushing through the barriers that have you fenced into your current reality. You need to learn how to unlearn everything that you have used until now. When you do this, you will learn a way to find the new you and your new capacity to achieve greatness.

This next step is going to be a little confronting because you are going to come face to face with all of the things that have been holding you back all of these years. It is important that you give yourself enough time to carefully consider this exercise and come back to it as many times as you need to in order to overcome all of the obstacles that are in your way. This is a mindset exercise I facilitate once every three months, and I use it to set the direction I will take for the next ninety days in both my life and my business.

Go somewhere quiet with no distractions. Bring a notepad and pen so that you can write down what comes up when you ask yourself these questions. Make sure you repeat them as many times as necessary until you have nothing left to write down:

What is stopping you?

Where did it come from?

Why is it getting in your way?

Once you have this, I want you to write a number next to each of these limiting beliefs in order of which ones you feel are having the most impact on your being unable to achieve what you want. This will be the list you will use to tackle each of these items one by one with the tools I am about to give you.

Tell yourself this:

All the things written on this page are beliefs, not truths. I will not accept them as my reality, and I will do everything in my power to change them.

Your beliefs are yours and yours only. So, if they are in fact yours, then they are also yours to change and adapt to suit yourself. As the author Evelyn Waugh wrote, "When we argue for our limitations, we get to keep them."

With that being said, do you really want to keep all of the things written on your page? Do you want these beliefs to become your reality and determine the course of the rest of your life or the lives of the generations that follow you? Are you willing to do what is necessary to create meaningful change?

Look at each of those limiting beliefs you have written on your page, and ask yourself the following:

What if the opposite were true?

What if these negative beliefs could be turned into positive beliefs?

What if my turmoil could be converted into strength?

This needs to be a process of reframing the obstacles into tools that can be used to craft your new future. For example, you can say that your financial struggles have helped you raise awareness around the life of abundance you really want, that your eighty-hour-a-week job has shown you how much time you really want available to enjoy your life, or that your separation from your partner has given you insight around how you can be a better father to your kids. I want you to reframe each and every single limiting belief, as hard as that may be, into something positive that gives you hope and reflects the reality you want in your life.

With this positive mind frame around each of these beliefs, immerse yourself completely in each one. Accept each of them as your new reality, as 100 percent truth, as if you had known all along that this was your belief and as if you had held this frame for years and years. You need to tell yourself with 100 percent confidence that each of these frames that you have now told yourself are yours. This action is how you will reframe every limiting belief you will have between now and the rest of your life.

You will turn your turmoil into prosperity.

You will turn your struggle into success.

You will turn your hard work into the life you desire.

You will turn your financial stress into financial freedom.

You will leave a lasting impression for generations to come.

You will break the cycle, and life as you know it will be better.

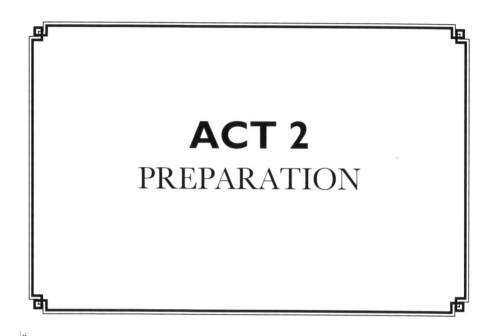

# ACT 2
## PREPARATION

CHAPTER 5

# Packing the Right Tools: The Foundations (Part 1)

Have you ever heard the saying, "You can't build a house without having solid foundations"? I'm sure someone in your life has preached this to you over and over throughout the course of your life. In response you probably thought, "Yeah, thanks for that, mate. I will keep that in mind if I ever build a bloody house!"

I am going to preach the same thing to you because when it comes to the foundations of wealth, nothing is more important than getting these right before you do anything else. Let's talk about why the foundations of wealth are so important and why you need to allocate as much time as you can to perfect these steps before you do anything else.

I am going to put this into context. What better analogy than to talk about building a house (surprise, surprise!)

You have bought a beautiful piece of land that you have been wanting for a long time. It has the perfect aspect, it's in a nice neighbourhood, and you are excited to build the house of your dreams. You and your family start thinking about all of the details you are going to include, like a big, open kitchen with an island in the middle, stone benchtops, good appliances, an alfresco dining area—the list goes on. I am sure you would want to plan down to the last detail to ensure everything was exactly as you wanted it, because you worked so hard to get to this point, right?

Do you really think about the foundations or what goes into the process of allowing you to obsess over all of the small details? Unless you are a builder yourself, probably not. You leave it to the specialists to make sure that the house is strong, complies with the rules, and will be a structurally sound home for years to come. So why is it that we don't obsess over the foundations of our dream home with the same passion as the benchtops, appliances, or that much-needed parents' retreat?

Well, that's because it isn't sexy or exciting, is it!

The foundations are boring and basic, and they lack the details that allow us to get our juices flowing. It isn't until something goes wrong with our foundations or our foundations hold us back or prevent us from doing the exciting stuff that we invest any time or effort into it.

For most, the same holds true for the foundations of wealth. Most of us go through life without paying enough attention to getting the basics right before we dive face-first into the sexy parts of wealth creation. The truth is that the boring stuff is what really makes the difference. When it comes to anything in life, I follow a tried-and-true three-step self-assessment that I want you to adopt into every part of your life, because this is what the most successful people in the world use to assess any key decision they look to make:

1.  Is it simple? Can I explain and understand it easily?

2.  Is it sustainable? Can I stick with this long term and make it a part of my life?

3.  Is it scalable? Can it work regardless of how big or small this gets?

I want you to apply this to everything you learn in this book when you consider your current situation in contrast to what I am telling you to do. I know you are going to think that it's too much work or it isn't going to add much value. But I ask you to objectively question how you do things now and ask yourself if it truly ticks all of the three questions above. With this and along with the tools I am going to give you, your life is going to change, because I am going to get you more excited about your foundations than you have ever been in your entire life!

Ambitious claim? Let's get started.

The foundations of wealth come down to six key areas of your financial life that will be relevant for the rest of your life. These will be the core values that you will pass onto your kids to set them up with the best foundations, which will stand strong no matter how big any of you choose to build your tower. Remember, the deeper the foundations, the higher you can build.

These six areas are broken up into Plan A and Plan B, both of which we have broken down across two chapters. They are as follows:

**Part 1 | Plan A**

1. Cash Flow
2. Household Debt
3. Lifestyle Planning

**Part 2 | Plan B**

4. Emergency Funds
5. Protection
6. Estate Planning

These six key pillars that form your foundations will allow you to systematically review, assess, and revise the key parts of your wealth journey. They will ultimately determine your financial success and allow you the freedom to build the house of your dreams.

I bet you are rolling your eyes already in boredom, thinking, "Jackson, you have lied to me. I thought this was going to be the most exciting thing I have ever done."

Please try your best not to drift into an endless slumber while I dive into each of these subjects and explain what role they are going to play in changing how you do everything in life from here on out. Not only am I going to help you alter the course of the rest of your life, I am also going to give you a step-by-step guide to setup your foundations so that you have more free time and more money to build and grow.

In my experience, having great support and guidance from like-minded people increases the likelihood of your success, so we have created a support group on Facebook called "The Wealth Mentor Reader Support Group." We would like you to join the group and share your progress, questions, pains, and gains with the group. My team and I will make ourselves available in the group to answer questions, provide guidance and support, and ensure that you get everything you need to take action and pursue what you really want.

## Cash Flow: Cash Is King!

I *hate* budgeting—always have, always will. I am sure you cringe at the idea of doing a budget. Having to work out what I spend every month and plug it into a spreadsheet only to see all of the mistakes I've made seems like a fruitless task. I am sure you totally agree.

Why do we all hate budgeting so much? Well, it stems from the idea that we have to attempt to sacrifice the things we want to buy day to day to inevitably fall short of what we were aiming to achieve. Of course, some of us are fantastic budgeters who are willing to eat cornflakes for dinner to pay off the home loan in five years. I am definitely not one of those people. And from my experience working with thousands of clients, I know most of you aren't like that either.

You want to enjoy a coffee in the morning. You want to enjoy that nice steak dinner with a good bottle of wine on a Saturday night. You want to drive to work in a nice car and take a nice holiday to the Bahamas once a year. I am no different. In fact, as I write this book, I am sitting in a beachfront apartment on a beautiful island in Brazil called Florianopolis. We all want the finer things in life that make all of our hard work worth it, and we all want to have our cake and eat it too.

Well, can't you have both? Can't you enjoy all of the fruits of your labour while planning for the future? I believe 100 percent that you can if you have a plan.

My life's motto is "live for today and plan for tomorrow." We need to ensure we give equal effort to both areas if we want to be successful. The cornerstone of this is our cash flow and understanding how we can allocate our available resources—that is, manage our cash flow—in order to achieve our desired objectives.

So, what exactly is cash-flow management? Cash-flow management is the process of understanding exactly what comes in, what goes out, and what is left.

Simple, right? Well, most of us never get a handle on this simple process. I will explain why.

There is no magic to building wealth. It all starts with cash-flow management. In order to build wealth, we need to spend less than we make and use that surplus income to invest into assets that appreciate in value. How most people tend to go wrong is that they tend to spend first and save whatever is left, which, for most of us, is a number between bugger all and nothing.

A valuable lesson is taught by a book called *The Richest Man in Babylon*, which is a series of parables about those within the ancient city who have been able to amass serious wealth and the secrets to their success. The key learning that I pass to my clients is "Pay yourself first."

What does that mean exactly?

When the poor Babylonian quizzes a rich man about how he made his wealth, the rich man gives him very valuable advice.

"I found the road to wealth," he says, "when I decided that a part of all I earned was mine to keep. And so will you."

This fundamental mindset is about making the conscious choice to shift from being a consumer to being an owner and retaining a piece of everything you earn first and foremost, then spending what is left.

Ask yourself, is this something you do each and every pay cycle without question? Do you have a fixed percentage of your income that you put away for the future before you choose to spend even $1? The harsh reality is that most of us go through life never adopting this. This ultimately determines our fate of achieving a mediocre financial outcome and maintaining a state of survival.

Why do you think the government takes your taxes from you before you receive your wage? Why do you think the ATO starts taking tax instalments if you are self-employed? It's because the government knows that as humans, we are inclined to spend what we have and live within the means we have available. Even with this being said, one of the areas many of my business owner clients struggle with is managing their tax debt. And in Australia, they aren't alone, with over $35 billion in unpaid taxes being owed to the ATO.

This goes to show that when it comes to cash-flow management, you are not alone.

Ok, Jackson, I get it. I need to pay myself first and save before I spend. But how do I put this into practice?

Good question, and I will get to that in due course. First, we need to identify the problems before we look to implement a solution.

In an age of technology, cash-flow management has become even harder. We have the unlimited convenience of facilities like tap and go, paying from our phones; endless credit card offers; points cards; buy now, pay later deals—and the list goes on. The industry of consumption goods has made it too easy for us to blow all of our money on rubbish we don't need, and it allows us to expedite the process of receiving instant gratification from our spending behaviours.

Trust me—this is a well-thought-out master plan to keep you in a never-ending spiral of material things funded with bad debts that allow the corporations to get richer as you struggle to keep your head above water.

Sounds grim? Well, it is the reality of far too many Australians, and things need to change.

With this unlimited scope for you to spend your way to consumer ecstasy, what can you do to escape the clutches of modern-day society? You need to have the right weapons to battle against temptation and become the richest man or woman in Babylon!

As a consumer, you likely fit into one of a number of spending profiles, and I am sure that at least one will resonate with you:

## The Cash Stasher

You live a comfortable life, but you don't have any assets that appreciate in value or provide you with passive income. You have nice things, go to nice places, and don't have much, or any, debt to worry about. But everything seems to track along month to month with no real progress other than maintaining the status quo. You are too scared to invest—

"just in case" you need the money—and tend to stockpile cash. You fear the market and have likely moved your superannuation to cash or a conservative investment option in case another global financial crisis rolls around.

## The Cash Splasher

You love to throw money around, shout drinks! at the bar, pay for dinners, and treat your friends to nice things on their birthday. You see yourself as generous and always want to give to those around you to ensure everyone has a good time when you are around. You are good at saving toward things that are important to you. And when you have your mind set on something, you will do whatever you have to in order to save for it. You enjoy big-ticket items that make you happy and make you feel good, but you seem to lack motivation unless you have the next big thing in sight.

## The Cash Makes Me Happier

You love a bit of retail therapy, and the solution to all of the world's problems exists either in a shopping mall or on your favourite online store. The feeling you get when you leave the shop with a bag of new goodies or see the postman come with a package in hand is second to none. And you are on a first-name basis with all of the sales assistants, who can see you coming from a mile away.

## The Chicken Little Investor

You really enjoy investing and spend your time obsessing over the *Financial Review*, the finance news, and every world event that triggers a spike or crash in the market. You spend more time than you would like in your share trading account, buying and selling with every new piece of information you have at your disposal. Whether you want to admit it or not, after taxes and fees, you know deep down the market is beating you black-and-blue with underperformance and losses. You tend to lose track of how much you have actually made and only speak about the great decisions you have made when bragging to your mates.

## The Points Accumulator

You love a good bargain and will go out of your way to do anything that will score you a freebie. You are always hunting for the next points scheme and hoard them to get the free flight, cheaper groceries, or VIP tickets to the premier of the latest Marvel movie. You spend time comparing your utilities providers online and will switch and negotiate a better deal every couple of months to save a few bucks. You want to be in complete control of your finances. You check every bank statement and grocery bill to make sure that nothing has gone amiss or that you haven't been short-changed.

## The Ignorer

You were off to a good start, but somewhere along the way, things started to spiral out of control. You accumulated debt and seemed to use one credit facility to pay off the next one. Now you can't seem to get ahead and seem to use all of your surplus to try and pay the minimum repayments on your cards. Now you bury your head in the sand, avoid opening bills out of fear, and try to forget about the financial reality you are experiencing every day. You can't bear to make strategic decisions to try and get ahead, and you would much prefer to defer this by distracting yourself with absolutely anything else.

## The Midas

Everything you touch turns to gold, and you know that money will keep on flowing. You earned more this year than last year, and you know next year will bring even more. You live a life of what you believe to be abundance. But it seems to be only lifestyle abundance, not financial abundance. You want to start planning, but there is always next year, as you are too busy having the time of your life living the dream.

Personally, I am an impulse spender. If I obsess over something and tell myself I want it, I will do absolutely anything in my power to have it. This has been a pattern I have followed for most of my adult life up until a few years ago when the penny finally dropped for me and I started developing my own "Values Based Advice" model, which was honestly a way for me to sort out my own problems first and foremost and use this as a case study to help my clients.

Once again, this reality for me was something I learned from my parents, and this survival was something my own survival depended upon. My mother was an ignorer and spent most of her adult life as a hard-working hairdresser who never knew much about money management. Luckily for her, she never accumulated much debt. But I remember as a child seeing piles of unopened letters on the table from banks, utility providers, and the like, and I could never understand why.

"Mum, why don't you open your letters? Aren't you curious what they are about?" I asked naively.

"I already know what they are, so there is no need to open them," she responded before quickly changing the subject.

This process of burying her head in the sand was the way she learned to cope with the reality of her financial situation. Although she worked hard and never seemed to spend on extravagant things, there never seemed to be enough money to get on top of her financial commitments.

In contrast, my father was always very disciplined with his finances and always tried to teach me values of getting ahead financially. He always taught me to open bills as soon as I got them and pay them before the due date. He always taught me to try and live within my means and to save for a rainy day, which were things my father always did well.

Another thing my dad always did well was accumulate meaningless crap. In turn, he never had enough money to buffer the effect of the unforeseen.

Our house was always filled with little odds and ends, trinkets, antiques, and other belongings that my father accumulated over the course of his life. At one point he had accumulated so much that we were unable to park a car in our two-car garage, because it was filled literally to the ceiling with items he had purchased and managed to stack Tetris style until there was literally no room left.

After spending years trying to convince him to clear out the mess, I remember spending an entire weekend sorting through every item to get his approval before we chucked it out on the council clean-up, which happened twice a year in our neighbourhood.

"Dad, can we chuck this out?" I asked as I held up every item one by one.

"Nah, nah, nah. I might use that," he responded about every single item.

You can imagine how the story went from here and the uphill battle of trying to convince him to part with his beloved collection. I persevered, and we managed to make enough space to fit one car diagonally as long as all the passengers got out of the car before entering the garage.

Great success! Not really.

My father's inability to save for the future and just survive led him to nearly bankrupt himself when he was diagnosed with aggressive stomach cancer at the age of fifty-seven. With no financial means to fall back on and no means of protecting his ability to remain as the key breadwinner, he survived by using personal loans and credit cards and by redrawing on his home loan while he battled to recover from having one foot in the grave. He did get better, and he managed to live another nine years before the cancer finally took him, but he was never able to recover from the devastation the original event had on his financial situation.

I had my own personal battle with consumerism that I fought from when I was old enough to get a job. I have literally lost track of the obsessions I created one after the other that led me into a cycle of always spending all of my money in pursuit of accumulating things that really held little material value after the initial appeal wore off.

My biggest spending failure was the start of my first business. It was a men's fashion label called Siete Clothing Co. I had been working for NAB as an adviser, and due to a restructure, I was docked around $20,000 per annum in remuneration, which, at the time, was a big hit to me. My father was suffering from cancer, and I was trying to supplement his living expenses and help cover the mortgage while he was trying to get back on his feet. His fourth wife had left him, and I was all he had left, so I needed to find a way to bridge the gap I had experienced. My brilliant idea at the time was to start a fashion label from scratch.

Now, anyone who knows me would know that I love business and that I live and breathe entrepreneurship. I believe that anyone who is good at what they do should work to be self-employed. If you look at the wealthiest entrepreneurs across the world, most of them became wealthy by starting their own business or investing in business.

So, you are probably thinking "Jackson, aren't you contradicting yourself here?"

Well, not really.

You need to get into business for the right reason. The right reason is one of the following:

1.  You are passionate about what you do and live and breathe it.

2.  You want to help people find a solution to a problem.

3.  You are an expert in your field and you want to leverage this to its fullest potential.

I was none of these things when it came to fashion. I was 100 percent motivated by making money to supplement my and my family's lifestyle, and I had no intention to be any of those three things.

Money is not the destination. It is the fuel that helps you get there.

So, fuelled by greed and my ego, I spent the next three years, hundreds of thousands of dollars, and countless hours trying to get a business off the ground while working fulltime as a financial adviser with my only objective being to find a way to make more money for myself.

What happened?

The business failed, and I found myself in around $100,000 of debt, with personal loans and credit cards coming out of my ears. With all of my efforts to try to break the cycle and not end up like my father, I found myself in the same situation as him but only earlier in life, just trying to keep my head above water.

How could I have let this all happen? How could I let it go so far? Despite all of the knowledge and experience I had as a financial professional, I was unable to use it to my advantage.

Life has a habit of consuming us and allowing us to be caught up in the complexity of day-to-day life. It seems that before we know it, the landscape around us changes, and once we escape the trance we are caught in, it is all too late.

So, what did I do?

I'd like to say I cut my losses and moved on with my life, but it wasn't that simple. To be honest, I shut down the business. But, with my head buried in the sand and the door closed, I kept all of the inventory stacked to the ceiling of my spare room as if it were a tribute to my dad's hoarding days. It wasn't until last year that I decided to close this chapter of my life. I donated all of the inventory to charity. It was finally time to accept my loss and move on with my life.

I hope this story resonates with you and shows that something seemingly small and harmless can snowball into something severe if given enough time and fuel to compound to an uncontrollable size. The sooner we can come to terms with our flaws, the sooner we are able to make a conscious decision to make a meaningful change. My first mistake was not having a good understanding of my cash flow. And as I tried to find solutions to my problem, I made it worse before it spiralled out of control. I am thankful that I have tackled all of my bad debts and used this negative experience as fuel to create one of the world's best cash-flow management processes, which has allowed me to advance my wealth and my clients' wealth exponentially.

Let's get back to you. I am going to give you a step-by-step guide.

## Step 1. **Profit and Loss Statement**

As you can see from my experience, it is important to understand your current situation so that you can identify problem areas that exist in your cash flow. This step is about coming to terms with what you earn, what you spend, and what should be left over at the end of each month. Now, I can't stress enough how important it is to be honest with yourself here, as this is the first building block to renewing the relationship you have with money.

Now, with as much detail as you can possibly think of, you are going to fill in an Excel spreadsheet with all of the figures. We have created one of the easiest spreadsheets you can use as your template in order to get all of those numbers in one place so that we can assess your current position.

But Jackson, isn't this a budget? I thought you said we were never going to do one of these!

No, it's not a budget. This is your profit and loss statement for your very own company called "Your Life Pty Ltd." You are the director and

CEO of this company. As the visionary, how can you ever hope to push forward in pursuit of your goals if you have no idea where you are?

Convinced yet? Perfect! Now, let's get cracking.

You are going to go to our website book.wealth-mentor.com.au, and there you will be able to create an account to our book support portal where we will provide you with supporting tools and some great resources that include the spreadsheet and detailed instructions around how to complete the task.

We have attempted to make the spreadsheet as user-friendly and interactive as possible, and the aim of the exercise is to understand a number of key areas, which I will explain below:

**Income**—Is your income purely derived from employment, or do you have passive income sources? Additionally, do you receive discretionary, bonus, or commission income that is irregular, and how does this affect your cash flow?

**Fixed expenses**—The necessities of life that are non-negotiable and unlikely to change.

**Discretionary expenses**—The nice-to-have things in life that add value to your lifestyle and tend to vary.

**Surplus**—Once all of the above has been considered, how much should you have left over?

This is our first reality check to come to terms with our current situation. When possible, ensure you work with your significant other to complete this task, as it is important you are both fully vested in this process.

## Step 2. Damage Control

You have your profit and loss statement completed. You have reviewed it multiple times to make sure that nothing is missing and that the numbers are as accurate as possible, regardless of how good or bad they may look. Your next step is to consider the following, which will ultimately determine your next steps:

1.  Do you have a cash-flow surplus? If so, does it match how much you have leftover in your bank each month on average?

2.  Are you happy with your level of cash-flow surplus, and do you believe it is enough to allow you to achieve your goals?

3.  If you have a cash-flow deficit, or more going out than coming in, can you identify where the key issues are?

Damage control is a vital stage of your future planning, so we have put together a damage control cheat sheet on our member portal. Make sure you go and watch the module on

## Step 3. Structuring Your Accounts

I know you will say, "But Jackson, I have a great account structure, and I can't be bothered changing my accounts, which I have had since I was five years old, as that's too much hassle." Too bad! This step is an absolute non-negotiable, and I will explain why.

For most people, the reason they have absolutely no idea about their cash-flow position is that they have no clear separation between their various expenses and their lack of structure, ultimately leading to inefficiencies in their cash-flow management, overspending, and less-than-expected surplus. Over the course of my career as an adviser, I have seen the use of an appropriate cash-flow structure increase surplus on average of 40 percent for a household, which is huge!

Let's say, for example, your current budget surplus is $10,000 a year. If we were able to increase this by 40 percent to $14,000, and assuming we invested that surplus into something that returns 8 percent per annum, the difference would be $490,000 over thirty years!

I know it will take you a few hours of work, but do you think it will be worthwhile for a potential $500,000 return on investment? I hope so!

Let's talk about your current structure for a minute and find out what is going wrong. Most of us fit into one of three buckets:

## 1. The single account sinkhole

You have one account that is most likely an account you have had for as long as you can remember. You have all of your income coming in and all of your direct debits coming out automatically. And you spend all of your money using your debit card, regardless of what the expense is. You save what is left at the end of the month (maybe). And from time to time, you find you have to dip into this account to protect against things that come up unexpectedly or that you forgot about.

## 2. The credit card crusher

You love your credit card, and you use it for everything. You believe the points are the best thing since sliced bread. And you believe the more you spend, the more you earn. You either pay your card off religiously each month and swear by the fact that you never pay interest, or you are caught in the cycle of endless interest, balance transfers, and deferring your ability to get ahead financially. Either way, you aren't saving to your fullest potential, and your credit card company loves you for it.

### 3. The transfer technician

Your online banking app is your favourite app, and you have more accounts than you know what to do with. You have your little stash pots of funds for everything under the sun, and your saving strategy can be compared only to the hibernation ritual of a squirrel preparing for winter. You seem to constantly transfer money backward and forward between accounts, standing at the checkout while a fifteen-year-old kid looks at you funny before you swipe your card to buy groceries.

Seem familiar? Thought so. I have seen it all before, thousands of times, and you aren't alone. To be completely honest, I was the credit card crusher, and I used to tap and go my life away without ever thinking of the consequences of my actions. Before I knew it, my card was maxed out, and I always felt so out of control. So, I found a solution that worked for me and has worked for countless numbers of my clients and other financial professionals to whom I have taught the same process.

# BUDGET STRUCTURE

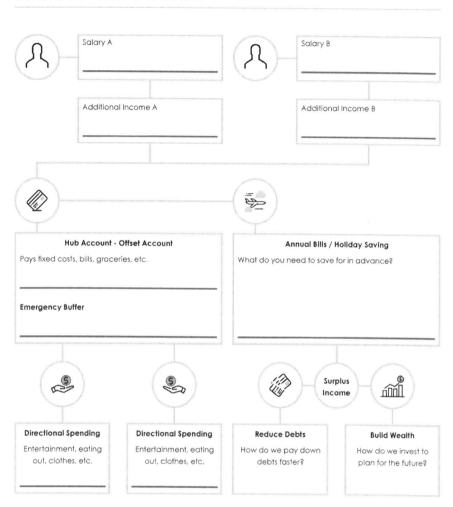

Figure I

The idea of this structure is to segment your spending into buckets. Each bucket has a collective purpose of putting you in control of what you spend. In my experience, for most of us, the problems don't exist in the fixed costs, such as groceries and the necessities of life. They normally exist in our personal spending, which may include coffee in the morning, dinners out on the town, entertainment, and that nice pair of shoes you could never go without.

We have all been there, and it is a matter of trying to put the right safety nets in place to stop you from going astray. This is about giving yourself a weekly allowance that reflects a comfortable lifestyle in which you are conscious of those three self-assessment questions we spoke of before and in which you tick the sustainability box. This isn't about eating cornflakes for dinner or sitting at home like a hermit eating ramen noodles and watching Netflix. This is about deciding how much is enough to allow you a comfortable life within your means while leaving you enough to build and grow.

Let's discuss all of the accounts and what they are for. You should ideally need three accounts for a single and four accounts for a couple, which are as follows:

**Hub account**—This is your key operating account, and all money comes and goes via this account. The purpose of this is to position your cash flow as if you were running a business and allow for you to see everything that comes and goes from a central location. All of your fixed expenses or non-discretionary costs, such as mortgage, rent, utilities, groceries, or the non-negotiables, will come from this account.

**Annual bills and holidays**—This is an account for you to save for things in advance that will sneak up on you. You want to average the total annual cost as a monthly amount so that we can establish an automated transfer to put money away for this. By doing so, you will avoid having to chuck this on your credit card and then try pay it off for months afterward.

**Personal spending**—This is for any item that is discretionary, such as your Netflix subscription, morning coffee, entertainment, clothes, and so on. This is the tough one, as I know most people have no idea what they spend here. Ideally, you want to break this down to a weekly amount so that you can drip-feed yourself money and look to form fresh spending habits.

Now, if you are setting this up with your partner, you need to ensure that you take away any potential fuel for disputes. Stats show that the primary reason for separation or divorce is arguing around financial issues, so I am committing to you now that once we set this up, you will eliminate most of these issues immediately.

First, you and your partner get the exact same amount of personal spending. It doesn't matter if one of you earns more than the other. You are in a partnership, and you need to work together. Decide on a fair number that works for both of you, and set this up as an automated transfer to each of you weekly. We will talk about how we review and fine-tune our cash flow shortly.

So, this is what I want you to do:

1. Go to our member portal book.wealth-mentor.com.au, download the budget structure diagram shown above, and fill it in. If it is easier for you, draw it out on a piece of paper. I want you to use your profit and loss statement to fill in all the boxes.

2. Put in all of your fixed expenses as a monthly average figure, which will give you an idea of how much will be deducted from your hub account each month.

3. Work out your total annual bills, such as car registration and annual insurance, along with your annual holiday budget. Break this down into a monthly figure.

4. Try your best to collate all of your personal spending for the year, including coffee, eating out, entertainment, clothing, and other nice-to-have things. Break this down into a weekly figure.

5.  You are going to average out your surplus into a monthly figure. With this plan, this is the magic number we are going to work with to help you achieve your goals.

Now you are probably asking, "Jackson, you haven't told me what I should be saving yet! What does a healthy surplus look like?"

Well, that is a very good question and something of hot debate for a long time. Senator Elizabeth Warren, when lecturing as a bankruptcy professor, was famously quoted using the 50/30/20 rule, which teaches that you should use 50 percent of your income for necessities, 30 percent for discretionary spending, and 20 percent for saving. That sounds fantastic in theory but doesn't always work in practice.

In my experience working with over one thousand clients, I have never encountered two people with the same cash-flow situation. Everyone is in a different life stage, with different incomes, expenses, kids, illnesses—you name it. So how can we apply the same principals to everyone without first considering their situation?

My answer to this question?

Save as much as you can comfortably afford in your situation, and make sure it passes the three self-assessment questions:

1.  Is it simple?

2.  Is it sustainable?

3.  It is scalable?

The best course of action is to establish a fixed amount of savings every month that you can use to form a habit, systematically review it each month or so, and increase it slightly while working to reduce the costs you have in another area. These small adjustments over time will result in huge compounding and help you work toward what is really important.

## Step 4. Setting Up Your Accounts

Now, I know this is the part you will probably dread, but it needs to happen. Look at this as a short-term pain for long-term gain. I know that once this is in place, you will be on your way to having the most solid foundations that can exist.

First, this structure will differ depending on if you are a homeowner, so I will break down a guide for each of you to ensure you get the right direction.

## Non-homeowner

As a non-homeowner, your objective is to try minimizing your bank fees, which will erode your savings, and to maximize any small amount of interest you may get, although given globally low interest rates, this is unlikely to make you rich anytime soon. I want you to find out exactly what your bank has charged you across all of your accounts for the last twelve months, and you can achieve this by giving the bank a quick call. If you have multiple financial institutions, I want you to make this call to all of them. Yes, I know this is painful, but it serves you right for having multiple accounts across various institutions! It's about time you get on top of it.

Believe it or not, there are financial institutions out there that offer $0 fee accounts, regardless of the balance, and even cover the costs of your drawing money out of random ATMs at two o'clock in the morning. Sounds too good to be true, right? Well, you just haven't been looking hard enough.

The one that I myself have used and tested in the past is ING Direct. They have offered great accounts with no fees, fully featured online access, ability to transfer between accounts instantaneously, and decent interest on their savings accounts, which don't require you to have a PhD in astrophysics to understand the fine print and terms and conditions around their interest policies.

The downside is that ING does limit the number of accounts you can open. This can limit the structure you can set up, so ensure that you work out what allows you to set things up best for your situation.

Please note that I have no affiliation with ING Direct, nor do I receive any commissions or fees for recommending them to my clients. I position myself as a strictly fee-for-service adviser, and I only receive remuneration from adding value to my clients, so rest assured that I have your best interests at heart!

The good news is that you can setup your accounts online with little effort and start the ball rolling.

What I want you to do before switching accounts is to conduct your own research and compare the options, such as ING Direct or any others you find using a comparison site, like CanStar, finder.com.au, or InfoChoice, that will allow you to assess the pros and cons, especially when compared with your current accounts before you make the switch.

Once you decide, it is now time to pull the trigger. Here is what you are going to do:

1.  Open a hub account, which will be a transaction account with a debit card attached. If doing this with your partner, make it a joint account.

2.  Open a personal spending account, which will be a transaction account with a debit card attached. If doing this with your partner, setup one each in individual names.

3.  Open a bills and holiday account, which will be a savings account. If doing this with your partner, make it a joint account.

Simple as that! Apply for your accounts, wait for your debit cards, activate them, and now it's time to start cooking with gas!

## Homeowner with a Mortgage

As a homeowner with a mortgage, you need to get money working for you instead of working for the bank, and there are a few creative ways you can do this. First, are you using your current transaction accounts as a way to offset the interest you pay on your mortgage? This is one of the most powerful ways you can get money working for you without the risk of investment volatility, and I will explain to you how:

Let's assume you are earning $80,000, which results in a marginal tax rate of 34.5 percent. You have a mortgage with an interest rate of 4 percent, but you need to pay this interest rate after you have paid tax. Assuming your mortgage is $500,000, your annual interest repayment would be $20,000.

How much have you actually had to earn to pay the $20,000?

In this scenario, you would actually need to earn over $30,000 to then pay your tax to pay the bank its $20,000. This results in your effective gross rate of earnings to pay your loan of 6.1 percent!

Now ask yourself, is there anywhere else where you can receive a 6.1 percent return on your money with zero risk? Considering that interest rates in Australia are currently 1.5 percent and savings accounts give you less than 3 percent, I think not.

For all of my homeowner clients, I use a facility known as an offset account, which operates like a transaction account, offers a debit card, and has the added bonus that any money that sits in that account even for one day will reduce the value of your loan for the calculation of interest.

For example, if you had $50,000 sitting in your offset for a year with a loan of $500,000, you would only pay interest on only $450,000, which would reduce your interest for the year by $2,000. Not bad, huh?

So why does the bank offer this? Well, more often than not, they know the convenience of the offset account leads more consumers like you to overspend and take longer to pay back their loan. Unfortunately, this is the harsh reality for many homeowners using an offset account. But I am not going to let this happen to you. Do you know why?

You have the benefit of having the world's best account structure to help you manage your cash flow like a boss!

So here is the plan:

1.  Contact your mortgage broker and discuss your current loan structure. If you don't have one, get one, as mortgage brokers are the best way for you to get objective advice and compare all of the products on the market.

2.  Look at a provider that will give you access to multiple offset accounts that will allow you to establish the banking structure outlined above.

3.  If your current bank does this and offers a competitive interest rate, fantastic! Make the arrangements immediately. If not, arrange for a refinance of your current loan to a provider that gives you this.

4.  Establish an offset account for your hub account, bills and holidays, and personal spending for both you and your partner. If you are joint holders on the mortgage, this will result in all accounts being joint.

## Step 5. Transferring your expenses

What we need to do now is the trickiest part. We will need the help of your existing bank for this. The hardest part of transferring your banking is shifting all of your debits across to the new account, so I will give you a step-by-step guide to make it as easy as possible for you.

1.  Get your employer to update where your pay goes, and provide them with your Hub Account details.

2.  Contact your existing bank, and ask them for a list of all of your current direct debits or the last ninety-day statement where most of your bills come from.

3.  Highlight all of the ones you will be keeping, and contact your service providers with the new details of your hub account. Ensure all future payments come from there.

4.  For any bills you want to get rid of to create more surplus, call each biller and ask them to cancel your direct debit from the file, and check that you are not in a contract and that you are within your rights to cancel.

5.  Ensure you keep a balance sufficient enough to cover anything that may be missed so that you can come back and do damage control as needed.

6.  Once you are confident all of these debits have been shifted, close your accounts with your old banks, and go celebrate with a drink or two.

This process of using your own money might be a shock to the system. I am sure that some of you are freaking out right now, worried about direct debits being missed and bills not being paid. I understand where you are coming from. Many of us who rely on credit to get by and smooth our cash flow will find it hard to get this established, so here's what I want you to do.

The first thing is that we need a buffer to ensure we don't struggle to keep afloat in this transition. We want to ensure we have enough in both the existing account and the new account for the first month or two as we get used to this new structure. For this we need to have around one month's fixed expenses in cash split equally between the old account and the new account to get us by.

But Jackson, where the hell am I going to find that?

Well, you need to put your thinking cap on. Can you sell some stuff on Gumtree, offer your services to a friend for cash, or busk in the street? Whatever you need to do, you need to get this money together and make a conscious decision to break the cycle and start making some real progress. This isn't supposed to be easy. I promise you that once you put in the hard yards, it will all pay off.

## Step 6. Leveraging Technology

Although technology has resulted in creating so much convenience that it is easier than ever to spend, it has also resulted in some amazing solutions that help us leverage the above structure to understand how we are spending and ensure we are on track toward what we really want. As discussed previously, transparency is the key to success because we need to know where we are in order to know where we are going. As such, we need to leverage technology so that we have complete oversight of how we spend and how this spending affects how we progress toward our goals.

An abundance of solutions are on the market. We have done all the hard work to review them and ensure you have the best possible solution that gives you all the features you need to keep on track for your financial goals. Remember, your cash flow is really the centre of wealth creation, and it is really important that you get this right. Once you have this down pat, you will be in a position to create the life you want in the way you want it, and you will be able to make informed and educated decisions regarding your future.

So, with that being said, our preferred solution is MyProsperity, an Australian company that specializes in cash-flow management and future planning software solutions. Their solution gives you access to

- automated data feeds from all of your bank accounts, credit cards, and loans;

- automated data feeds from most superannuation and investment products;

- reports on the value of your property and vehicles;

- projection tools to allow you to calculate how you are tracking toward your goals;

- collaboration with your other financial professionals; and

- document storage on the cloud.

This tool is aimed to provide you with a central hub to give you access to everything you need to have complete control over your finances. You get all of this for $25 per month!

So, with the power of all of the above, we need to work out how we use it to get the most out of your spending behaviours in order to help you get where you want to go. We have created a step-by-step guide to help you get up and running with this new technology and set you up for success. But you need to take the first step.

This is what I want you to do:

- Jump online to our book portal at book.wealth-mentor.com.au

- Watch the section on cash flow management and download the guide.

- Contact us to get setup with your MyProsperity account.

- Follow the steps to get set up with your data feeds and link bank accounts, assets and liabilities.

- Once completed, post your progress on the Facebook group and celebrate simplifying your cash flow.

Once you have your technology set up, I need you to make a commitment to yourself, because we need to make all of this hard work worthwhile. I know that most people see technology as a fad, become obsessed with it for a while, and then get bored, get over it, and forget about it. We cannot allot this to happen here, because the technology adds no value if you don't use it regularly to review, revise, and refine.

So here is what I need you to do:

- You are going think about your weekly schedule and work out a night of the week that you rarely have anything on. Choose a night in which you will have little disruption and an hour to just think about yourself. If you are doing this with your significant other, make sure you can both be available at this time.

- Once a month on this night, you are going to have a recurring meeting to order your favourite food, open a nice bottle of wine, and review your goals.

- Set this in your phone calendar as a recurring meeting for yourself, or you and your partner, indefinitely called "Financial Freedom Night."

- You are going to commit to never making excuses or deferring this meeting, and you are going to promise to make this a lifelong habit of working on yourself.

- With your Financial Freedom Partner, you are going to watch the video on the portal to get you started.

If you don't have an accountability partner I want you to reach out in the Facebook group and find someone like you to partner up with. I know this might be a daunting experience, but accountability is a big part of achieving financial freedom. Get yourself out of your comfort zone as we are all in this together. Working towards financial freedom doesn't need to be a lonely journey and we are here to support you in pursuit of success.

# Household Debt: Destroying Your Debt

*Debt* is a word we are taught to fear as children. More often than not, our fear consumes us to the point that we ultimately end up with a dysfunctional relationship when it comes to debt. I have seen more people than I want to admit become slaves to debt and spend their lives in an endless battle to overcome it. In contrast, I have seen many of my clients become masters of debt and use it to build substantial wealth using the bank's money while using the power of leverage to turbocharge their trajectory toward financial freedom.

So, what separates these two very different groups of people and their experience when it comes to debt? Well, it ultimately comes down to how they choose to magnify their situation, either for better or worse.

I want you to look at debt in a different way, and I want to help you understand where to draw the line to ensure that you never fall into a situation where your debt consumes you. In any situation, debt is extremely risky. Even the most seasoned investors have been crippled by overextending themselves, expecting that property and share markets would continue to rise, only to experience some kind of market correction and lose everything. With that being said, I don't want you to fear debt. I want you to respect it and use it only when you have understood the significance of your decision and how it will help you along your wealth journey.

I remember that as a high school student sitting in math class, I had a teacher who was the first person to teach us about debt. It was a memorable experience because, to this day, I cannot comprehend the logic of her explanation to us. In this class, she was explaining to us the value of a credit card and how she used it for everything under the sun.

"It's fantastic, and you can accumulate these things called points! You can use these points to get all of this great stuff, like flights and holidays, for doing nothing but spending on what you were going to buy anyway!" she proclaimed proudly in front of our entire class.

"But why would they give you stuff for free? How do they make money?" someone asked, trying to make sense of it all.

"Well, the banks think that most people are just going to spend too much and not pay it back, so the bank makes interest. I guess they work it out so the things they give away are less than the interest most people pay," she responded confidently.

"So, do you pay interest, Miss?"

"Well, of course not! I wouldn't be a very good math teacher if I did that! The bank doesn't want you to do this, but I have my pay deposited directly into my credit card, so I know I never need to worry about it."

What did she just say? She puts *ALL* of her money onto her credit card each pay? I still cannot believe it.

I swore to never use a credit card because it sounded all too dangerous to me (that obviously didn't last long, because I like to live dangerously!).

So here we are as school kids getting taught about consumer finance from someone who has a completely dysfunctional relationship with money, and we are pushed out into the world expecting to know how to conduct ourselves properly? I think not. I have a huge gripe with our education system, which allows corporations into our schools to teach our kids financial principles that are all for the purpose of grooming them for a life of bad debts and monstrous interest repayments.

I bet you all remember the Dollarmites program run by CBA when you were a kid, right? That account that your mum would give you some money each week to put into that little collection bag to teach you how to save? Do you remember how much you got back when you left school? Well, after fees and poor interest, you got something between diddly-squat and F-all! Think back to when you turned eighteen, and try to remember the mail that was sent to you. Do you recall there conveniently being VIP offers from the big banks to share their generosity and give you a brand-new credit card with a pre-approved limit much higher than you could possibly afford? Where did you think they got your details, birthday, and other personal information?

My point exactly! These big organizations profit from your lack of financial literacy, and these are the ones responsible for educating our kids about money. Something needs to change.

## Good Debt versus Bad Debt

I am sure you have heard before that there is a difference between the debt you have and that there are good debts and bad debts. To explain this further, let's define each one:

A bad debt is a debt that has been used to buy something that depreciates in value or does not provide you with an income. This includes any spending on your credit card, car loan, personal loans, mortgage on your home. This is a bad debt because it is not tax-deductible and has not been used for anything that advances your wealth position.

I bet you home owners are already saying, "But Jackson, my home went up by forty percent, so why is my mortgage a bad debt?"

Well, it's fantastic that your home went up in value. Your home is a fantastic asset, and kudos to you for getting to that stage of your life, but the money is locked up in your house, and that increase is not working for you unless you unlock that equity and use it to build your wealth or generate more income.

So, let's give you a reality check to talk about what your bad debts are actually costing you. Similar to how we did that interest calculation we did before, we will do the same for all of your bad debts. Let's assume you earn $80,000 and pay around 34.5 percent in tax. So, what this means is that you need to earn money and pay tax to then pay your interest bill to the bank.

I am going to assume the following interest rates:

Mortgage—4 percent

Car Loan—6 percent

Personal Loan—13 percent

Credit Card—20 percent

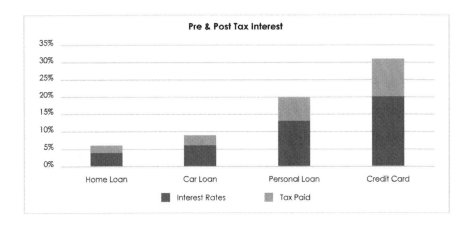

Figure 2

I want to make this real by putting some numbers around this. Let's assume your debts are as follows:

Mortgage—$500,000

Car Loan—$30,000

Personal Loan—$30,000

Credit Card—$30,000

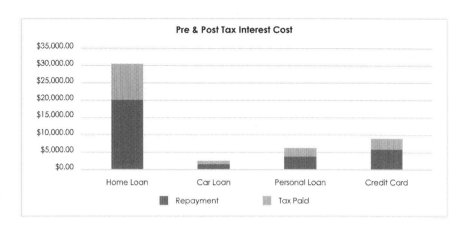

Figure 3

As you can see, the interest rate has a significant impact on what you are required to earn in order to meet your repayments, which is why so many people suffer the effects of their debt as they struggle to earn enough to pay the interest and start tackling the principle. How do you feel about having to earn over $30,000 a year just to pay the interest on your mortgage? I hope this is an eye-opening exercise.

What I want you to do is line up your bad debts, and we are going to tackle them one by one. We want to start with the highest interest debts, and we will work our way down. This is about devoting your 100 percent concentration on eliminating as many of your bad debts as possible using the power of the cash-flow structure that you have setup for yourself.

Here is your action plan to smash your debts to pieces:

1. Get a list of all of your bad debts and include the latest balance, the current interest rate, the minimum monthly repayment, and the total you paid in interest last year as a dollar amount.

2. You are going to order them from the highest interest to the lowest.

3. You will cut up all of your credit cards minus one, which you will keep in your bottom drawer at home until you have enough emergency funds to cut it up too.

4. You are going to maintain the minimum repayment for all of your debts, and if you are currently paying more, adjust it as soon as possible.

5. As soon as you have your emergency fund to a value of $5,000, you are going to divert all of your surplus into the highest interest debt. At this point you will cut up your last card and celebrate.

6. Work out what your surplus is each pay cycle, and on the day you get paid, this amount of surplus will be setup to be paid automatically to your highest-interest debt.

7. Calculate how many pay cycles it will take you to pay off the highest interest debt.

8. Once it is paid off, close the account. When they offer you more credit, tell them where to stick it!

9. Rinse and repeat.

You might be asking, "Jackson, why don't I just balance transfer my debts and not pay interest?"

Well, this is an option, but it is a dangerous one. It's like going to the casino and putting all your chips on black. You have a chance to win and have your bet pay off, but there are no guarantees. Why do you think the banks offer this service? I'll tell you now that it's not because they are trying to do you a favour. It's because they are the house at the casino, and they know that the odds are stacked against you that you will transfer your debt, ride the wave of the 0 percent interest, and then get hit with an extremely high rate.

They win. You lose.

Think about it objectively. Can you trust yourself with transferring the balance on your debt, cancelling your own card, cutting up the new one, and paying off the debt *IN FULL* before the interest-only period expires?

If you said no or maybe, don't do it!

If you hand on heart can say yes, then make sure you have your cash-flow structure in place, and follow steps one through nine above exactly the same, only tackling this 0 percent interest card first. If you use this strategy, please make sure you shop around to find a bank that will not charge you balance transfer fees or other charges and that gives you enough time to tackle the debt in full before the rate expires. Good luck!

Now let's talk about good debts. Good debts are those that we use for the purposes of building wealth. Typically, this debt will be used either for investment property or for shares, and the interest you pay is tax-deductible. Good debts are how many successful investors leverage their cash in order to control more wealth with the aim of having compounding exponentially grow their wealth. Good debt is not all fun and games, and as I mentioned before, many seasoned investors have gone broke from overextending themselves.

In Australia, typically, most of us will use good debt for the purposes of buying an investment property. And as Australians, most of us live and breathe property and want to live the Australian dream by accumulating as much bricks and mortar as we possibly can. This property mentality has led to huge growth in the property market over the last forty years, and many of us have done extremely well off the back of this boom. It is important to understand that investment markets don't always go up, and we find ourselves getting caught up in the bright lights of other people's fortunes before we dive in feet first at the wrong time. The time prior to the global financial crisis was no exception, and many people were chasing astronomical investment returns of 20 percent to

30 percent every year only to buy into the top of the share market and experience 40 percent to 60 percent losses in one year.

We are getting ahead of ourselves a little here, but we will come back to wealth accumulation later. One thing I will do here is quote the wise words of arguably the best investor of our time, Warren Buffett,

"Be fearful when others are greedy. Be greedy when others are fearful."

When we are talking about good debts, we need to consider the reasons why we would use debt to advance our financial position, and it is all about compounding. Compounding is the process by which the capital value of your investment increases. In this process, as the capital value increases, the asset value snowballs over time through exponential growth. It is important to note that compounding can also occur in the opposite direction.

So, let's look at the power of compounding using leverage for a moment. Let's assume you have $100,000 saved and want to use it to acquire property. Borrowing limits and stamp duty aside, let's look at how powerful long-term compounding can be when used in conjunction with leverage over ten years. For this example, we have assumed an average annual compound rate of 5 percent.

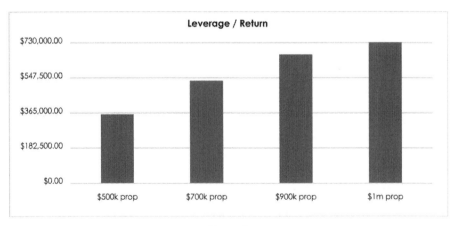

Figure 4

As you can see, the higher the leverage, the higher the potential return on your money. Seems simple, right? Well, not really.

When it comes to good debt, many people overlook the key factors that erode your return. We need to understand this if we are ever going to use debts to positively impact our financial situation, so let's do a crash course on our key considerations when using leverage to invest.

Our key points to consider are:

1.   What are our repayments, and can we afford them?

2.   What is the interest rate, and what happens if it goes up?

3.   If the asset value falls, can the bank force me to sell my investment?

4.   How long am I prepared to wait in order to make a positive return?

5.   What are the factors that could land me in hot water and make me unable to pay my debt?

We need to understand that whenever we use debt, whether it be good or bad debt, it magnifies the potential outcome of the situation. Debt should be used with caution, even when buying good assets as it has a direct link to cash flow and in turn, can have a significant impact on your lifestyle if you do not carefully consider the risks before diving in. Additionally, when we have good debts, it is always best to have an asset that is positively geared- meaning that it produces more income than the expenses, as opposed to having an asset that is negatively geared- meaning the costs exceed the income received. Although Australia has some of the best negative gearing rules in the world, it is always better to have more money in your pocket than having something that takes money away from you, even if there are some tax incentives involved.

We want you to be successful with your household debts so we have worked to build some helpful videos, activities and worksheets on our member portal at book.wealth-mentor.com.au so please jump on there and ensure you work through this as it will help you get clear on what you need to do.

## Lifestyle Planning

You are probably overwhelmed after thinking about debt for so long, so now it's time for some more exciting stuff. This is what we refer to as *lifestyle planning*. The whole idea behind this book is to help you create the life you want for you and your family, so this topic is something that is close to my heart, and I expect it is a significant motivator for you to read this in the first place. Our lifestyle goals are the lifeblood of why we work so hard and sacrifice in order to live the dream, so let's talk about the key lifestyle goals we need to consider as part of our financial foundations.

Remember, the foundations are the pillars on which the rest of our financial plan is built, so we need to have peace of mind and certainty that we are on track for our core lifestyle goals before we look to reach for the stars. In my experience, the key lifestyle goals that form our foundations are

1. owning your home, and
2. living from your passive income.

These two goals are key milestones for our wealth journey, and for most of us, they are the epitome of making it financially in life. I want you to work with me so that we can define what you need to achieve these goals at a really high level, and we will work together to reverse engineer a plan that you can follow to achieve them both.

Priority number one is owning your home. If you already have achieved this, fantastic. And congratulations, once again. If you have your home but you want to upgrade to something better, we will discuss this at length later on. You might ask, "But Jackson, why is owning my home so important when you said we need to use bad debts to buy it?"

Great question!

Stability is an important part of financial freedom, and owning your own home outright is a significant part of having stability in your life. Let's fast forward and think of you in retirement as a seventy-year-old. Your landlord decides to sell the place you are renting. Do you really want to pack up all of your things and be at the mercy of the rest of the rental pool to find a new place only for it all to happen again? I thought not. Our home is our nest, and it will form a positive asset base that can be used later on for wealth creation or, if needed, can be downsized tax-free to assist you with funding your retirement.

Although we need to use bad debts, we are wired in such a way that we work best by paying things off as opposed to saving for something in advance. Thus, acquiring your own home is a form of forced savings that is locked away for safekeeping, out of your reach.

Before we set out in search of our dream home, we need to work out what we can afford, because many first-time home buyers tend to get caught up in the emotion of the experience and overextend themselves. When it comes to property, we need to consider not only what we can afford now but also what the impacts of interest rate increases can do to our budget. The last thing we want is for you to sacrifice everything you have worked hard for!

So how do we work toward getting you into your home? Let's work out what it is likely to cost you.

The first step is determining your affordability when it comes to having a mortgage, which will in turn help you define a budget of what you can afford to spend. It is not uncommon now in Sydney to see people spending over 40 percent of their household income on just their minimum mortgage repayments, which presents a significant risk if rates start to go up. Given that we are at historical low rates, it is only a matter of time before this happens.

If you are renting, I want you to multiply your weekly rent by fifty-two to obtain your annual rent cost, and divide this number by your total net annual income. This will give you what percentage your current rent is of your total income.

An example of this is as follows:

You pay $500 per week in rent, and you and your partner both earn $80,000 a year. You will pay a little over $19,000 in tax, leaving you with $61,000 take-home pay each.

500 x 52 = $26,000,
$26,000 ÷ $122,000 = 21%.

You can use this as a point of comparison for your mortgage repayment, which we will calculate for you shortly.

Experts say that ideally, given the risks associated with interest rate fluctuation, you shouldn't spend more than a third of your income on your mortgage. So, considering the above scenario, you need to ask yourself how you would feel paying close to $41,000, or nearly $300 extra a week, to have your own home. This will obviously come down to your cash-flow situation and your ability to create surplus.

The idea of this exercise is to reverse engineer your cash-flow capacity before you start looking for your dream home. I bet that as soon as you see the place with the kitchen you want, the nice courtyard, and the parents' retreat, these numbers will go right out the window. So, we need to do the hard work how to keep you on track.

So now we are armed with these two numbers: our current rental spends and 30 percent of our household income. We are going to go back to our profit and loss statement, which should have all of our new figures in there from all of the expenses we have negotiated, our new personal spending limit, and everything else clearly reported. I want you to save a new version of this document called "dream home cash flow," and this is what we will use to work out our likely position when we put together our plan to get your own home.

Exciting, right?

We are now going to put our proposed numbers into the budget to see how it looks, so I want you to take out your rent from the spreadsheet and enter in your new mortgage repayment. What does this do to your surplus, and does it allow enough additional funds available? Do we have around 20 percent of your household income still left for future planning?

Once we have this, we are going to work out your budget for your purchase. At the time of writing this book, most home buyers with a 20 percent deposit could find themselves securing a rate around 4 percent. So, for the purposes of this exercise, we will use this for our calculations.

In the calculator you are going to enter in your interest rate and your monthly affordability, which we calculated previously. This will give you an idea of what size loan you can afford. For example, the above household with $122,000 net income can afford a loan for around $700,000. Assuming the household has a 20 percent deposit and stamp duty, it could acquire a home for around $875,000.

What we also need to consider is the impact of interest rate increases on your affordability, so I would like you to run the same scenario considering interest rates of both 1 percent and 2 percent higher than your current rate. This will allow you to understand what this does to your cash flow.

Let's consider the example of the couple earning $122,000. If they purchased their $875,000 home and their $700,000 mortgage went up to 5 percent, this would consume almost 39 percent of their income. At 6 percent, this would account for over 41 percent of their income. As you can see, the impacts can be significant depending on their surplus position.

With this future affordability calculator, we are able to work out whether you can afford to weather the storm of future rate increases and how this could be absorbed into your budget. The last thing we need to factor into our affordability analysis are the costs of holding a property, which is something many people overlook.

When buying a property, we need to consider the costs of council and government fees, strata rates for units and townhouses, water and other utilities, and general maintenance and upkeep. As a general rule of thumb, we like to assume a rate of between 1 percent and 1.5 percent of the value of the property to cover for these things. Using the above example of a property worth $875,000, we would want to consider the costs between $8,750 and $13,000 per annum as a guide. Make sure you factor this into your profit and loss.

The math is now done, and we need to review our numbers. We have our affordability calculations and the expected costs of owning our home. We have also considered the potential impacts of interest rate increases. Once we have this, we are now able to get to work with mapping out our plan!

First, let's work out how long it will take for you to save your deposit. As a general rule of thumb, we always want to save 20 percent of the proposed property we want to purchase. Yes, we can borrow more than 80 percent of the value, but this will generally incur an insurance called Lenders Mortgage Insurance, which is basically a policy to protect the bank if you default on the loan. This can cost around 2 percent of the value of the property and is not tax-deductible if you are planning to live in your home.

As an example, for an $875,000 property, if you wanted to borrow 90 percent of the value, the premium would be around $17,000!

There are other ways to speed up the process, but we will talk about them later.

For the purposes of this exercise, we are going to work out how long it will take you to save this deposit and not factor in any interest or earnings you can make. The reason for this is that your rate of return will really depend on where you invest and for how long, so we will come to this in the wealth creation topic.

I want you to calculate the 20 percent deposit of your home. We are going to divide this number by your monthly average surplus to work out how many months it will take you to get there. In the example of the couple with $122,000 in take-home pay, if they follow the 50/30/20 rule, we could expect them to have around $24,000 a year in surplus. In order to buy a home worth $875,000, they would need a deposit of $175,000. With their current surplus, it would take eighty-seven months, or seven years, to save this amount of money.

That's a long time, right? I feel your pain.

This is our reality-check phase, and I call this process "turning dreams into goals." In my experience, the only difference between a dream and a goal is having a plan to get there, so this is what we are going to create together.

We need to ask ourselves the right questions to set us on the path toward what we really want. This is never going to be easy, so we need to ensure we are ready for what's to come. Ask yourself the following:

- When you look at your number of months, how does that make you feel?

- Is that an acceptable amount of time to wait to get your home?

- If you want to get there faster, what needs to change now?

- Now, what do you really want?

I urge you to seek your own guidance at the time of reading this so that you can get accurate information about borrowing to buy your home. Most banks have a borrowing calculator on their website but for the most accurate assessment, it is best to contact an experienced mortgage broker. This is an ever-changing landscape and we advocate getting an expert opinion around this to help you plan. If you want to discuss your lifestyle planning, please reach out for a complimentary strategy session at www.wealth-mentor.com.au/contact and make sure you jump on our book member portal at book.wealth-mentor.com.au as we have created some helpful videos, activities and worksheets to help you with your lifestyle plan.

Priority number two is working out how we can get to the stage of life where we can choose whether we want to work. I like to call this the "pulling up stumps" stage (any of you cricket fans will understand the reference). This is when the game as we know it is over and we can live life on our own terms. Many of us refer to this as retirement, but I personally believe that *retirement* is a dirty word. I hate the idea of working my ass off until I am sixty-five just to never work another day; to sit at home, watching crappy daytime TV; and to go to the club to play bingo—please shoot me now.

My idea of financial freedom is being able to choose how I spend my time, whether that is lying on a beach in the Bahamas, sipping a coconut, or attending speaking engagements, trying to educate younger generations about how to reach for their goals. This time is about you and what you want, so let's try to work that out now.

We are going to dive back into your profit and loss statement. We are going to mould it into the desired state you want when you choose to wind down and live life how you want. I want you to remove all of the items that won't be there at this stage, such as debt repayments, rent, life insurance, and all other responsibilities that will no longer be relevant. I also want you to consider the lifestyle you want to be living, how much you would like to spend on holidays, how much your weekly entertainment spending will be, what clubs you will join, and so on. The more details you can include, the better.

Once we have this, we now have our desired-state budget, which gives us some insight into what our desired lifestyle will actually cost. The next part gets a little tricky, so we have tried to help out by creating an interactive calculator that allows you to play around with your ideas when you want to pull up stumps and with work out how much you need to be able to get there.

The logic of this calculator needs to consider the following questions:

- At what age do you want to stop working full-time?

- Will you continue working part-time? If so, how much will you earn and for how long?

- How much will your money make in returns per year (net of inflation)?

A lot of math goes on behind the scenes to do these calculations, and there are a few careful considerations we need to make today that will help us get a general idea of what we will need in order to achieve our future lifestyle goals. We like to refer to this as a *bucket strategy*.

So, what is a bucket strategy? Basically, it is a way for us to work out how much we need for each life stage in order to get where we want to go. We break this down into three segments:

Figure 5

**Short-term bucket**—Anything we need between now and the next twelve months.

**Medium-term bucket**—Anything we need from twelve months until age sixty.

**Long-term bucket**—Anything we need from age sixty plus.

Why is age sixty so significant? Well, in Australia, based on current legislation, this is the earliest age that we can access our superannuation tax-free, and this is a really big deal. Think about it. Imagine an investment that allowed you to keep 100 percent of every return you got, and imagine drawing down an income without having to share any of it with the government. Well, this exists, and you likely have money in there already!

Most of us couldn't care less about superannuation, and I know it receives a really bad rap in the media, but we are lucky to have one of the best superannuation and retirement schemes in the developed world. I am going to give you a simple, no-BS crash course on superannuation to get you onboard with how it can help you live a tax-free retirement, because there is currently no other way you can avoid the taxman in your later years.

I am going to fast-forward for a minute and show you the power of superannuation in retirement, based on the current rules, compared with the alternative. I am also going to illustrate the impact that tax can have on your retirement plan. For this example, I am going to assume that you have $1,000,000 in retirement savings, your returns are 5 percent per annum, and you draw down $50,000 a year from your savings and start from the age of 60. Assuming your average tax rate outside of superannuation is 21% compared to the 0% inside superannuation, your superannuation money would last until around age 88 compared to only 83 outside of superannuation just because of the additional tax you would need to pay.

As you can see, the impact of taxation is huge and can result in your hard-earned money being eroded away, leaving you short. This could have been entirely avoided if you only had your money in the right structure. The important point of the bucket strategy is the direction in which we consider our goals, as it is important that we don't neglect any bucket. But it is also important to consider that we shouldn't put all of our efforts toward the long-term bucket if that causes us to fall short of our goals between now and then. As we know, nothing in life is certain, and there is no point in sacrificing everything for a future that we might not be around to enjoy.

So, our job is to ensure we have enough in each bucket to allow us to do what we need within that time frame. And then once those goals are achieved, we progressively tip our buckets over into each other to ensure they always have enough inside to sustain our journey. With a well-thought-out bucket strategy, you will always ensure you have the resources you need to live the life you want.

Lifestyle planning is about getting really clear on what you want, what you need to get there and what action needs to be taken to keep you on track. Jump on the member portal at book.wealth-mentor.com. au and download the worksheets that will help you start mapping this out and taking action.

CHAPTER 5

# Packing the Right Tools: The Foundations (Part 2)

I hear this all the time: "I don't have enough time to look at my plan B yet. I barely have enough time to do plan A!" I get you 100 percent. This is your mind's internal defence mechanism protecting you from being overloaded with negative thoughts, emotions, and the old "she'll be right" statement that normally results in you overlooking these things.

The harsh reality is that bad shit will happen, and there is nothing you can do to avoid it. You can, however, put strategies into place to help you reduce the impact and ensure that a bad situation doesn't mean the end of the world as you know it. Plan B is about not burying your head in the sand, accepting that life will throw us curve balls, but we can reduce or even totally avoid the impact of these bad situations with the right planning.

Plan B is all about taking the time to consider the 'what ifs' if your financial life and considering what you can do to protect what you care for most. I want you to approach this seriously as this is one of the most important parts of this entire book and I have seen first-hand where the right Plan B can change lives for the better, or lack of a proper Plan B can bring everything crashing down around you and your family.

This is not a scare tactic, merely a caution to ensure you give this section the attention it deserves so you have the right foundations to support your journey.

## Emergency Funds: What if the Wheels Fall Off?

We all hope for our plan A to go as expected, but life has a tendency of throwing curveballs at us, which can cause us to drift off track or force us to stop entirely in pursuit of our goals. I have seen all too many get caught off guard from the unforeseen and struggle to endure the situation just because they lack resources to buffer the impact of these kinds of situations.

In my experience, most people don't plan for these situations. And when they do occur, most people tend to rely on bad debts to get them out of a bind, which ultimately delays their ability to work toward their financial and lifestyle goals, which is less than ideal.

There is a simple solution, and having emergency funds available at all times helps protect us against these situations that can catch us off guard and push us off course from where we ultimately want to go. These situations can be anything from unexpected car breakdowns outside of warranty, medical emergencies, repairs to your home, or anything in between. The fact is that most people bury their heads in the sand and expect that these kinds of situations will never happen to them. But more often than not, Murphy's Law tends to prey on those who are underprepared.

So how can we solve this? Well, let's think about what could happen.

- Think about any emergencies you or your immediate family have had in the past and what they cost.

- Put yourself in a situation that you think could happen to you in your current situation, whether it be loss of job, hot water system blowing up, family member overseas getting sick, or whatever. What would you like to have available in this situation to ensure you don't need to take on any bad debts?

- Now, are you willing to wear this risk or save enough to buffer it? Or can you transfer the risk into someone else?

Transferring risk isn't about pushing this onto another family member or friend. It is about whether you can outsource the risk to a company who offers you insurance against the particular event. We will cover this in the next topic. But in most cases, this is for risks that you cannot save enough to protect against or that would be so detrimental to you and your family that it is best to mitigate the risk through options outside of self-insurance.

I always try to keep around $10,000–$15,000 in emergency funds at all times, as this has been the amount I have needed in the past to get myself out of precarious situations, and this has been true for a lot of my clients. I expect that many of you reading this book are expats from overseas, as a lot of my clients have migrated to Australia and have family back home. I have lost count of the times I have had clients have a family emergency and need to drop everything in order to book last-minute flights home. As you can imagine, this can cost anywhere up to $5,000 including accommodation and costs while overseas, so you can see how quickly your funds can disappear (or how quickly your credit card can get a serious punishing if you don't have enough emergency funding).

## Protection: What Can't You Do Without?

Protection is another area of most people's lives that is often overlooked, and this can result in devastating outcomes. Protection is about how we manage risk in our lives, and it is an extension of our emergency fund that often includes situations that we are unable to self-insure against. The key areas of protection are as follows:

- Assets—home, car, contents insurance
- Medical—health insurance
- Travel—travel insurance
- Lifestyle—life, disability, critical illness, income insurance

I list items in this order because it seems that most people tend to insure themselves starting from the top down. Most people whom I speak to cannot even fathom not insuring their car or home. But more often than not, they tend to overlook their biggest assets, such as their ability to earn an income, or even their life!

I 100 percent believe in insurance, but I understand that the industry as a whole carries a bad reputation. Much like superannuation, insurance companies have endured much persecution, with plenty of media coverage about the scandals of using technicalities to not pay claims and leaving families in need high and dry. I agree that there are bad eggs out there, but I will give you the tools you need to understand your risks, identify what coverage you need, and source the right companies or people to help you choose the right coverage for you and your family. As with anything, the process should be you first, strategy second, and product third.

When I started my career as a financial adviser, I worked as a risk specialist. As a fresh-faced nineteen-year-old, I was tasked with helping my clients, who were much older than I was, identify the risks that their situations presented and source the right insurance products to fill the gaps that existed. As a teenager, I really couldn't comprehend the risks, and I referred to a carefully crafted script, which my supervisor created, to ensure my clients were protected.

Pretty scary, right? Can you imagine getting advice from a nineteen-year-old around decisions that could impact not only your life but also the lives of your entire family? It's safe to say I carried a lot of responsibility on my shoulders. I was lucky that I had a number of great mentors, who taught me the ropes and showed me what I needed to do in order to protect my clients and give the best possible advice, and this mentorship has had a profound impact on many of my clients.

Once, I received a call from a lady who was looking for some life insurance, as she was heading overseas to Bali on a holiday. She was concerned about something happening and leaving her husband with the sole responsibility of managing their mortgage, and this was her main motivation for finding a solution. I remember taking the time to understand her situation and financial obligations, and I educated her around the different types of insurance she could consider.

As an adviser, it is my role to understand my clients' needs, educate them around the options, and advise them what I believe they need based on my analysis of their situation. In this case, the client needed far more than life insurance, and my recommendation included total disability coverage along with a policy known as trauma insurance (which we will talk more about later). After my explaining the reasons behind my recommendations and why she needed to consider these policies, she decided to act on my recommendations, which included around $1 million in life coverage and $500,000 of total disability and trauma coverage.

I guided her through every stage of the process, helped her choose the right provider, and submitted all the paperwork. We got the policy in place before she went on her trip. I didn't hear anything from her until three months later, when I received a call.

"Jackson, I wanted to let you know that I have just been diagnosed with breast cancer. I am not sure if that affects my premiums or if we need to notify the insurance company," she said, with uncertainty in her voice.

My client had a late stage of breast cancer that required a full mastectomy, chemo, and radiotherapy, but she was likely to make a full recovery. What she didn't realize is that the trauma policy we took out three months earlier covered for events such as cancer, and it was likely she would be entitled to a claim. I was able to guide her through the entire claims process and assist with all investigations. Within two weeks, I delivered a cheque to her for $500,000.

She couldn't believe that an out-of-the-blue call to someone who actually took the time to understand her situation and give her the right advice led to a life-changing experience. Shortly after finishing her treatment and making a full recovery, she was able to completely pay off her mortgage and was able to reduce her work to three days a week to enjoy more time with her grandkids.

I have processed more claims in the last ten years than I want to think about, but I am grateful that there is yet to be one instance of a client lacking money or having to endure financial uncertainty as a result of my advice. Unfortunately, this isn't the case for everyone, and I have had an experience that is very close to home for me that I still regret to this day.

My father was a blue-collar worker for most of his life and always enjoyed working with his hands. There wasn't much he wasn't able to fix, and he was always working on some home-improvement project in his spare time. My father was also a very smart man and one of the most well-read people I have ever met. His intelligence led him to try his hand in the professional world, and in the '80s he had a stint as an insurance and investment agent for AMP and National Mutual. From when I was a young age, he always told me stories of his success as a salesman and always preached the value of insurance. He also acted as one of my mentors when I started out as an adviser.

Not long after I started as a risk specialist, one of the senior advisers in the office told me that I needed to use my knowledge to ensure my family was protected. He told me that he systematically reviewed his own father's insurance every year to ensure that it was competitive and that it gave him the right protection. My dad was a stubborn man, and when it came to money, he would never take advice from anyone. When

I eventually found an opportunity to speak with him, I was met with very abrupt and confident responses.

"Jack, I used to do your job, so I know what I am doing. All of my cover is sorted, and there is nothing for you to worry about."

I wish I would have probed further, but unfortunately, you can't change the past.

My father was diagnosed with an aggressive stomach cancer in the early 2000s that almost took his life. He had never been sick in his life, and he always refused to go to the doctor, even when he was. After struggling to stay away from the hospital, he finally gave in after experiencing internal bleeding for weeks. He was immediately rushed into emergency surgery and was given a low probability of surviving beyond a few days. The doctors removed half of his stomach. Through the trauma of the operation and the subsequent recovery, Dad lost close to thirty kilograms.

I went to see him in the hospital. He was lucky enough to endure the operation, and it looked like he would pull through. The doctors said his road to recovery would be significant, with chemotherapy and radiotherapy. It was unlikely that he would be able to return to work for the next twelve months. My father was the primary breadwinner. Carrying a significant mortgage, we were all concerned.

"Dad, do you know your income protection details so that I can contact them and start arranging your payments while you are off work?" I asked him, curiously.

"Don't worry about it. I will deal with it when I get home. Everything will be fine," he responded as he usually did.

When he was able to go home, I finally convinced him to share the details of the insurance with me. I knew as soon as I saw the policy document that he was in big trouble. His insurance was titled "Credit Card Protection Plan" and was provided by his credit card company.

The policy provided him with relief from his credit card repayments for up to a maximum of $800 per month for a period of twelve months. It wasn't worth the paper it was written on, and my dad was in big trouble.

The next year was one of the most difficult of my life. I had to watch my dad try to keep afloat, keep our house, and provide for his family, which included my sister, who was still in primary school. This resulted in the accumulation of huge credit card debts, personal loans, and financial pressure, almost to the point of no return. He was lucky because his bank at the time allowed him to take a twelve-month repayment holiday while the interest compounded, and the debt grew.

The situation evolved almost overnight from being in a good financial position with a happy family to nearly losing everything. In twelve months, he nearly lost his home, separated from his wife, and lost contact with his daughter. He amassed close to $200,000 in bad debts and was forced to go back to work before he had fully recovered. The pressure of the financial burden hanging over his head was so great that I don't think he was ever the same.

Could this situation have turned out differently? I believe so. If only my father had taken out the right insurance coverage, allowed himself to take advice, and taken the time to identify the risks that existed in his situation, the outcome could have been very different. Unfortunately, I need to live with the "what if" of my reality, and this is what inspires me to ensure that you never have to endure the same.

## Personal Protection Crash Course

I want to give you all the tools you need to understand the four key areas of personal risk management that aim to protect your life, lifestyle, and ability to earn an income.

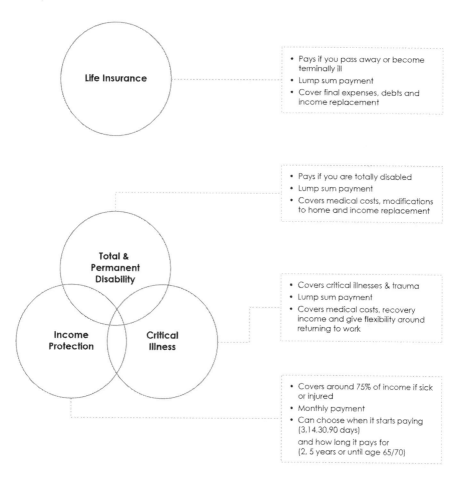

Figure 6

## Life Insurance

**What it is**—Life insurance or death insurance pays out a lump-sum benefit to your family in the event you pass away. Many life insurance policies also have a terminal illness benefit, which allows you to receive the money while you are still alive if you are unlikely to live longer than twelve to twenty-four months, depending on the policy.

**What I can use it for**—Your family can use it to pay off debts such as mortgage, draw down on the lump sum for replacement of income, or provide passive income sources for the family.

**What to consider**—In the event of your passing, what do you want to see happen regarding debt repayment, income replacement, and so forth?

## Total and Permanent Disability

**What it is**—Total and Permanent Disability coverage, or TPD, pays out a benefit to you if you are diagnosed with a sickness or illness that results in your being unlikely to ever be able to go back to work again. Depending on the policy, this could be just for your current job, or it could require you to be unable to perform any job you have had experience with in the past.

**What I can use it for**—TPD is often used to pay off bad debts such as your mortgage, provide for modifications to your home, cover costs of medical assistance and equipment, and replace income.

**What to consider**—If you were to be disabled and unable to ever work again, what would you want to see happen? Debt repayment, income replacement, medical costs, modifications to home, and so forth?

## Critical Illness

**What it is**—Critical illness, or trauma insurance, covers illnesses such as cancer, heart attack, stroke, and other serious medical conditions. Many policies cover upwards of fifty conditions, will pay upon your being diagnosed with a condition, and does not require you to cease working.

**What I can use it for**—Trauma coverage can be used for pursuing medical treatments that are not covered by Medicare or private health insurance. It provides the ability to take additional time away from work in order to take time with recovery, debt repayment, or enjoying quality time with your family.

**What to consider**—If you were to be diagnosed with a critical illness such as cancer, heart attack, stroke, and so on, what would you want to see happen regarding medical costs, debt repayment, income replacement, or lifestyle supplement?

## Income Protection

**What it is**—Income protection or salary continuance coverage usually provides replacement of between 75 percent and 85 percent of your gross income if you are unable to work because of injury or illness. Depending on the policy, you can select both the waiting period, which is the length of time you need to be disabled before getting paid, and the benefit period, which is the length of time the insurer will continue to pay if you cannot go back to work.

The waiting period can range from three days to two years, and benefit periods can range from two years up to age seventy.

**What I can use it for**—In most cases, income protection is there to replace most of your income while you are unable to work. It supplements your lifestyle and pays for your living expenses while you are unable to work. Some policies do carry other benefits, such as covering rehabilitation costs and providing other allowances, which vary from company to company.

**What to consider**—If you were unable to work for a period of time due to a sickness or injury, when would you want your income to be replaced, how much would you want replaced, and for how long?

## Structuring Your Insurance

Structure is something that is very important because it can have a direct impact on what you pay out of pocket and how you get paid if you ever make a claim. This is something often overlooked, and it is important to understand some of the tips and traps of insurance.

Typically, most people can choose to structure their insurance either in their own names, requiring them to pay the premium out of pocket, or they can choose to structure their coverage inside superannuation, which allows them to use their retirement savings to pay for their premiums. There are pros and cons to both, and we will review them as some food for thought.

## Table 1. Personally Paid

| | Life Insurance | TPD | Critical Illness | Income Protection |
|---|---|---|---|---|
| **Pros** | • Tax free to anyone who receives benefit<br><br>• Can be paid within 72 hours | • Tax free benefit<br><br>• Can receive 'own occupation' cover | • Cover only available when personally paid | • Tax deductible premium<br><br>• Generally more comprehensive cover |
| **Cons** | • Not tax deductible<br><br>• Consumes personal cash-flow | • Not tax deductible<br><br>• Consumes personal cash-flow | • Not tax deductible<br><br>• Consumes personal cash-flow | • Consumes personal cash-flow |
| **Summary** | Quick payment but may cause stress on cash-flow | Tax-free on payment and can allow for more comprehensive definitions but may cause stress on cash-flow | Only available paid out of pocket but it is quite often the most claimed upon policy | Catch all policy which is also tax deductible |

## Table 2. Superannuation Paid

| | Life Insurance | TPD | Critical Illness | Income Protection |
|---|---|---|---|---|
| **Pros** | • Tax deductible to super fund (paid pre-tax)<br><br>• Doesn't affect personal cash-flow | • Tax deductible to super fund (paid pre-tax)<br><br>• Doesn't affect personal cash-flow | • Not available inside super | • Tax deductible to super fund (paid pre-tax)<br><br>• Doesn't affect personal cash-flow |
| **Cons** | • Can impact your super balance and retirement savings<br><br>• Can take longer to process claim<br><br>• Tax free only to dependents (spouse or dependent kids) | • Only able to have 'any occupation' definition inside super<br><br>• Benefit is usually taxable | • Not available inside super | • Can be less comprehensive<br><br>• Can take longer to process a claim |
| **Summary** | Saves money out of pocket but could result in eroding super or tax being paid upon payment | Tax can impact the net amount you receive | Not available so not an option | May not give you the best cover and may take longer to receive benefit |

There is no hard-and-fast rule about how you are to best structure your coverage. More often than not, we use superannuation as a means of minimizing the impact to your short-term bucket while we work toward achieving short- and medium-term objectives. In turn, this allows us to work toward filling our long-term bucket faster and making up for any damage we did in the process.

Additionally, thanks to innovative insurance companies, we are also able to get the best of both worlds. This allows us to leverage the benefits of having coverage inside superannuation and fill in some of the apparent feature gaps we have through a process called *flexi-linking*. This is quite a complex structure, and we advise you to speak to a risk specialist about this option when you review your coverage. If you want to discuss your risk management plan or review what you already have, get in touch with us for a review.

## Stepped versus Level Premiums

I am sure you are familiar with the idea of your insurance getting more expensive each year as you get older. For many of us, we thought this was the only option we had. I have seen many a client take out an insurance policy but, because of rising premiums, ultimately have to reduce their coverage or cancel it completely due to affordability. Believe it or not, I have a business client in their sixties that has no choice but to pay over $30,000 a year in life insurance premiums. It is a significant compromise. But given their debt position, they would prefer to exchange the money for the peace of mind.

So, what if I told you that if you got in early enough, you could avoid ever finding yourself in the situation of having to choose whether to retain your coverage? Sounds too good to be true, right? Well, it isn't!

Around ten or so years ago, the big players in the industry invented a feature called *level premiums*. The idea behind this is that you get your insurance coverage in place early and lock in your coverage for age-based increases. This costs you more initially, but over time, the level premiums will be more cost-effective given that they do not increase as you get older.

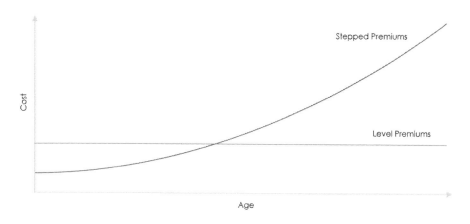

Figure 7

Now, we don't believe level premiums are for everyone, and there are a few key considerations you need to make before you decide on which way you will go:

- Depending on the policy, the crossover point is around nine years. Do you believe your risks are going to require you to retain coverage longer than that? For example, do you have young kids, a significant mortgage, and so on?

- Level can cost around 30 percent more when compared to stepped, so it is important you consider both the current comparable cost and the future comparable cost. Imagine the cost of stepped premiums in fifteen years' time if they continue to increase exponentially.

- In most cases, level premiums are only available until age sixty-five, so if you are older than your mid-fifties, it is likely that that level may not be worthwhile for you given your life stage.

- It is important you go with a reputable, high-quality insurer that offers the ability to pass back new changes that they make to their policies. This ensures you always have a strong policy as the industry continues to change.

Once again, there is no hard-and fast-rule here, but I tend to advocate that all of my younger clients consider level premiums, and this is how I structure my coverage. From my perspective, this gives me some certainty around my costs both now and into the future and ensures I will always be able to afford my coverage between now and age sixty-five. And when I compare this to stepped premiums over the next thirty years, I am on track to save over $100,000 in cumulative premiums, which is a big deal.

## Choosing an Insurance Company

Choosing an insurance company can sometimes be the most difficult task, but in a maturing industry with pressure for innovation, we are lucky as consumers that we are spoiled for choice. There are some very important considerations when choosing an insurance company, and they can generally be broken into two key areas: (1) quality and (2) cost.

As with anything in life, the saying "you get what you pay for" definitely runs true when it comes to insurance. I have seen far too many horror stories, which generally involve insurance policies that were cheap and nasty. I am not here to name and shame. I am here only to give you the tools you need to review and make an informed and educated decision as to the most appropriate coverage for yourself.

I will, however, give you a few tips for caution:

- Any TV advertisement that says, "get accepted on the phone" or "automatic acceptance" should raise alarm bells. An insurance company is not a charity and will not pay you without some kind of investigation. You need to ask yourself whether you want certainty around your ability to claim on a policy that you might pay into for decades that might potentially get declined or result in your family having to wait to get paid in a time of need.

- Many superannuation providers offer insurance when you apply that can cover pre-existing conditions, which is great. It is important to note that many of these policies decrease in value as you get older and may eventually cease all together.

- A jack of all trades is often a master of none. Your general insurance provider will often offer you packages to combine your personal insurance with them, but this often comes at the higher cost of compromise on quality.

All insurance companies will offer you two things until you are blue in the face: features and benefits. However, very few of them, if any, will actually advise you on the outcomes of these features and benefits or how they can help you in your situation. This is why it is so important to get the right advice, from someone who is in a position to give you the right guidance. To help you with this, we will give you a comprehensive checklist below to ensure you ask the right questions and get the right answers for you.

We believe that everyone should pay close attention to their risk management strategy and review it at least annually to ensure they have considered how their situation may have changed over time. Our ideal objective is to get into a position where we have enough wealth or passive income that we can choose not to have any insurance, but it is important to use an objective formula to assess this as you progress through your wealth journey. As you can imagine, having three dependent children and being the sole breadwinner carries more risk than being semiretired with no debt does, so we have developed a simple way for our clients to assess their risk.

Furthermore, it is important, once again, not to overcommit yourself to endless insurance coverage that consumes all of your surplus. It is all well and good to have peace of mind, but having that itself shouldn't cause you not to achieve your goals.

We have worked to create a needs and wants analysis that aims to help you ask the right questions and come up with some numbers around how much you would need in any of the above circumstances to protect what is important to you. The key thing to note here is that there are lots of variables to consider, an abundance of insurance companies offering different features and benefits, and endless ways to structure your coverage.

My motto with anything is to stick to what you know and outsource everything else, so it is important that you understand what you need and then seek professional help to get the right advice. A risk specialist is able to compare a wide range of product providers and ensure you are given the right advice as to which one is the most appropriate for you. Today, most risk specialist advisers operate with no fees for service because they receive a commission from the insurance company for their service. With industry regulation, most insurers should pay similar commissions, which aims to reduce conflicts of interest, but it is always best that you ask the right questions to ensure you are getting unbiased advice.

## Your Insurance Review Checklist:

1. Find all of your current insurance policies that you pay personally or have inside your superannuation, and request the latest policy documents from your various providers. book.wealth-mentor.com.au

2. Go to our member portal and watch the module to get clear on what you need to do

3. Complete the analysis and get an idea of your current risk needs before you go out in search of a risk adviser.

4. Give your adviser the details of your situation along with a copy of your needs and wants analysis. Allow your adviser to

provide you with the various options, quotes, structures, and details as to why they suit your situation. If you are concerned about something in particular (e.g., breast cancer or accidents at work), give your adviser this information so that he or she can find policies that best suit your needs.

5.   Consider the pros and cons of having your insurance inside or outside superannuation and of having it stepped or level.

6.   Request that your adviser provide you with a ratings comparison report that compares your current coverage with other products in the market. This will allow you to compare the features and benefits without having to review all of the product disclosure statements.

7.   Ask who your adviser holds insurance with and why. Good risk specialists should practice what they preach and be willing to share this with you.

Insurance and risk management is a necessary evil, and I urge you to consider your risk management strategy as early as you possibly can. For most, it can be set and forgotten and reviewed on an annual basis to make slight adjustments. Although it is a pretty grim subject, this is all about planning for the worst and hoping for the best. In my experience, it is better to have coverage and not need it than need it and not have it. One of my companies, Aureus Financial offers risk specialist solutions so if you want to get a second opinion or review what you have, get in touch with us.

## Estate Planning: How Do You Want to Be Remembered?

Another grim subject is estate planning and whenever I bring it up I see most people roll their eyes and say, "Oh yeah, that's been on my list of things to do but I haven't got around to it." Estate planning is an extremely important aspect of your wealth foundations, as it is generally another area you can set and forget once it is done. Estate planning is normally done in conjunction with your risk management plan and aims to clearly define what you want to see happen with your estate, or in other words everything you own or owe, and how you want it divided.

Your estate plan is broken up into five key areas that need to be considered:

## Binding Superannuation Nomination

**What it is**— One of the easiest estate planning mechanisms is a binding beneficiary nomination within your superannuation. For many of us, a significant amount of our wealth is held inside super when we consider both the balance and insurance. A binding nomination is a document that allows you to choose a beneficiary or beneficiaries to receive these funds and this document can simplify the process of these funds being paid out.

**What's included within it**— A beneficiary nomination normally includes the individuals name, address, percentage you wish for them to receive and their relationship with you. It is important to note that you cannot always make all people a binding beneficiary so please consult your super fund to confirm eligible beneficiary types.

Additionally, it is important to note that for a nomination to be binding, it requires signatures from two independent witnesses who are not beneficiaries on the same day you have signed it. Due to this, many beneficiary nominations end up being invalid and non-binding so ensure you do it right.

Finally, for many super providers they only allow for binding nominations to last for 3 years to ensure that you update them over time. Given that your wishes may change over time, this is meant to prompt you to review and update the nomination. More often than not, it is forgotten and once lapsed, it becomes a non-binding nomination.

Take some time to call your super providers and ask them whether you have a nomination, whether it is binding and if so, when it lapses so you can ensure you update it accordingly. If you want to setup or update your nomination, each fund has a standard form which they can email you or direct you to on their website.

## Will

**What it is**—Your will is a document that states your wishes of how you want your debts paid and assets distributed. It will nominate your beneficiaries whom you want to receive an inheritance state any other wishes you want to make in the event of your passing.

>**What's included within it**—There are a number of parts to your will, including the following:

>**Executor**—The individual or individuals responsible for interpreting your wishes, managing your assets and liabilities, dealing with tax and legal matters, and distributing your estate to your beneficiaries. The executor acts as a project manager to see everything through to completion.

>**Trustee**—The individual or individuals that can manage your assets on behalf of dependent beneficiaries who are unable to manage the money themselves. The trustee will make decisions around how the funds or assets are invested on behalf of beneficiaries or how they receive money based on their needs.

>**Beneficiaries**—The individuals who will receive proceeds from your estate. You will consider what they receive as either a dollar amount or a percentage, and you can place conditions around when they are able to receive their inheritance.

**Calamity Beneficiaries**—In the event of the worst-case scenario, and if your primary beneficiaries don't survive you, this aims to act as a backup to ensure you still have control over who receives your estate. This may be other family members, charity, or friends.

**Specific Gifts/Bequests**—If you own any items of significance, family heirlooms, or valuables, you can consider including this in your will to ensure these items go to the right person and in a legally binding way.

A will is the core of your estate plan and is something everyone should have, regardless of their asset position. The implications of not having a will can be significant and result in significant stress for your loved ones who will be required to handle your estate without the guidance of your specific wishes, which would have been included in a professionally written will. Most estate planning lawyers can finalize a simple will for you for a few hundred dollars.

## Testamentary Trust

**What it is**—A testamentary trust can be included as part of your will and is a legal structure that is created in the event of your passing that provides substantial asset protection and tax minimization benefits for your beneficiaries. A testamentary trust is normally a consideration for people who have a substantial estate (in excess of $1 million) or have financially dependent kids.

**What's included within it**—A testamentary trust is a way for you to clearly document additional wishes and provide guidance, particularly to the trustee of your estate, who may be managing money on behalf of young children. It allows you to have more control over theproceeds in the event of your passing. The key considerations are the following:

**Asset protection**—The trust allows for you to set an age at which your kids can get access to the money. This aims to avoid their making "spendthrift" decisions in their early adulthood. Additionally, you can provide guidance around the use of money, such as for education or wealth creation purposes.

**Creditor protection**—The trust can protect against events such as creditors or relationship breakdown of beneficiaries. This ensures that your beneficiaries and their lineal descendants are the only ones who are able to benefit from the inheritance.

**Tax minimization**—The trust does not have to distribute income to beneficiaries. This means that if your spouse or kids do not require additional income, they are not forced to draw funds from the trust and, in turn, are not required to pay personal tax on the money.

A testamentary trust can be a complex part of your estate plan, but it aims to give you more certainty and control over your estate on behalf of your beneficiaries. It is best to speak to an expert about this when you review your estate plan and discuss the pros and cons based on your current situation.

## Enduring Power of Attorney

**What it is**—An enduring power of attorney, or EPOA, is a document that allows you to appoint someone to act on your behalf for the purpose of dealing with your finances in the event you lose the mental capacity to make your own decisions. This person would be able to assist with managing your money, selling assets to fund treatment, paying bills, and anything else of a financial nature that is required.

**What's included within it**—An EPOA is aimed to ensure that if you were to lose capacity to make your own decisions, your finances could be managed on your behalf. Given the significance of this type of document, there are a number of considerations:

**Single or joint appointment**—Depending on your situation, you may feel inclined to appoint more than one person to the role to ensure that decisions are made jointly. You need to consider the complexity this may create, especially for basic tasks such as going into the bank to make an inquiry. You may consider placing restrictions on certain types of decisions requiring joint decisions to ensure your attorney is able to perform his or her role efficiently.

**Restrictions or limitations**—In addition to the above, you may wish to restrict your attorney from doing certain tasks, such as buying or selling property. Or you may require your attorney to seek professional advice for certain decisions, such as investing money on your behalf. Once again, it is important to consider that restrictions may cause your attorney to have difficulty performing his or her role, and once this document is put into place once you have lost capacity, it cannot be changed unless a court overrules your wishes, which can be costly.

**Deriving personal benefit**—Generally, most EPOA documents do not allow the appointed individual to derive personal benefit or be paid for his or her work. You may wish to consider whether you provide any allowance for costs he or she may incur as part of fulfilling his or her duties.

As this is a living document and would be enacted while you are still alive, it is important to consider who you appoint and how they are able to act. It is also important to consider appropriate backups if he or she is unable to assume his or her role. Once again, this is something that requires specialist advice and careful consideration before making a decision.

## Enduring Power of Guardianship/Advanced Health Directive

**What it is**—An advanced health directive is a similar document to the EPOA, but it appoints someone to make medical decisions for you if you were to lose the capacity to make your own decisions.

> **What's included within it**—An enduring power of guardianship, or EPG, is another significant document, and it aims to ensure you have the right people responsible for making key medical decisions if you are unable to act for yourself. The key considerations are the following:
>
> **Single or joint appointment**—Depending on your situation, you may feel inclined to appoint more than one person to the role to ensure that decisions are made jointly. This is particularly important for decisions that may need to be made that could determine whether you are kept alive in the event of a serious medical event.
>
> **Specific requests**—In addition to the above, you may wish to give your enduring guardian guidance around what you want to happen in certain events to reduce the pressure your enduring guardian feels regarding making the right decision. One consideration is how you wish to be handled if you are being kept alive by a machine, and you may consider including a "non-resuscitate clause," which would instruct your enduring guardian of your wish not to be kept alive.

**Deriving personal benefit**—Generally, most EPG documents do not allow the appointed individual to derive personal benefit or be paid for his or her work. You may wish to consider whether you provide any allowance for costs he or she may incur as part of fulfilling his or her duties.

This is a rather depressing subject. But having the right documentation in place can ensure your loved ones are given guidance around what you wish to happen in the event of the unforeseen and reduce the stress associated with these extreme situations.

We really hope none of you have to experience these types of situations, but we urge you to have these documents in place just in case. As such, we want you to take this off your list of things to do. And we want to make it as easy as possible for you to get this done with the right advice and at the right price.

Here's what you need to do:

- Go onto our portal at book.wealth-mentor.com.au and watch the "Estate Planning Review" section.

- Complete your instruction sheet.

- Make the time to speak to those you have appointed, and ensure they are aware of their responsibilities. At the same time, urge them to review their estate plan.

- With your completed instruction sheet, find an experienced lawyer who specializes in estate planning.

- Depending on your situation, the cost of this should be $300–$2,000 based on complexity.

- Ensure your documents are signed, witnessed, and stored safely, ideally with your lawyer.

- Keep a copy with the details of your lawyer and other financial professionals somewhere safe where your family knows where to find it.

If you need help with any of the above or would like a recommendation for a quality estate planning lawyer who can help you finalize the above at a reasonable price, please feel free to contact me.

## What You Shouldn't Do

There are some big no-no's when it comes to estate planning, and I want you to ensure that you don't fall into some of the common traps that I see with my clients, because they can be costly and cause substantial issues for your family:

- Don't use a will kit you find online or in the post office. These cheap options do not contain the scope for you to clearly articulate your wishes and can lack the legal credibility to minimize potential claims on your estate. It is best to spend a bit extra and get the right advice.

- Don't use services that charge you nothing upfront but hit your estate with a percentage management fee when you pass away. These seem great to save money upfront, but some charge upwards of 2 percent of your total estate, which can equate to tens of thousands of dollars that are taken away from your beneficiaries. Use flat-fee upfront services, which give you certainty around the costs involved.

- Make sure your documents are signed appropriately according to the guidelines of the law. I have seen many a will get drafted but never made official due to being unsigned or not witnessed properly.

- Make sure you review your will at least every couple of years. Things change, and it is important to dig it out and read over it to ensure it still reflects your wishes. Most lawyers will keep a soft copy of your documents, so if you change them, they will cost much less than the originals, given that minor changes won't take much time.

- Be clear and definitive. Estate law allows anyone to make a claim on your estate. If successful, they are able to pay for their legal costs from your estate. With many "no win, no fee" legal options available, there is very little to lose for people to try get a piece of the pie. You are able to protect your beneficiaries by getting your documents done professionally and ensuring what you want to happen is easy to understand.

This is the last part of your foundations, as it is often the hardest one to think about, but this is all about how you want to be remembered. It is important to understand that when your estate plan comes into effect, either you are no longer around, or you no longer have the capacity to fight your own battles. These documents can make the difference for your beneficiaries, so it is worth the time to get this right.

## Wrapping Up Our Foundations

Alright. So now you should have some really solid foundations, and that's a cause for celebration! These six parts of your wealth plan are some of the most important. By having them in place, you are now part of an elite few who have taken the time and invested the effort, and will be able to yield the benefits of this hard work for the rest of your life. This is what will set you up for success for the rest of your life and give you the peace of mind and certainty that you have a base that you can always fall back on in time of need.

Before we pop the champagne, I want you to check off and make sure you haven't forgotten anything:

- Check out our 'Wrapping Up Our Foundations' section on the portal book.wealth-mentor.com.au.

- Download the checklist and ensure you have followed the steps to reviewing and updating your foundations.

- Any items still requiring your attention, date mark them and ensure you share these dates with your accountability partner to hold each other on track for this.

- Share your wins with the Facebook group and if you need help or have questions please reach out to the community.

With all of this in place, I want you to celebrate and go enjoy something that has been on your to-do list for a while, whether that be going out to a nice restaurant, having a weekend away, or enjoying a nice day on the beach. Take some pictures of your achievements, and post them in the Facebook group to motivate others to do the same and join the club!

Remember, this is about living for today and planning for tomorrow. And all of this is aimed at giving you the tools you need to craft the life you want, so this is supposed to be celebrated. You deserve it!

# CHAPTER 6

# Don't Roll Backward: Wealth Protection

In my opinion, the best investor who has ever lived is Warren Buffett. In his lifetime, he has been able to grow his wealth from $5,000 at fifteen to over $80 billion at eighty-seven. Just thinking about the magnitude of this is a somewhat unfathomable feat to most, as the sheer size is somewhat difficult to comprehend.

As a wealth coach, I see endless investment consultants and fund managers preach about their unique approach to investing, their track history of performance. More often than not, most of them fall short of outperforming the index once fees and tax are factored in. Far too many investors have fallen into the trap of the active fund managers who charge excessive fees, catch you in their web of complexity and sophistication, and bring only lacklustre returns while putting dollars into their own pockets.

So, what does Warren do differently than most other investors or fund managers? How has he been one of the only active investors that has consistently outperformed the market year on year to build this huge portfolio of wealth and position himself as one of the richest men on the planet?

Warren has attributed his lifelong success as an investor to a few simple rules that he has followed religiously:

1. Rule number one—don't lose money. Rule number two—don't forget rule number one.

2. Be fearful when others are greedy. Be greedy when others are fearful.

3. Get around the right people.

4. Invest for the long term.

Furthermore, Warren is a risk management expert—the operative word being *management*, not *avoidance*. One of Warren's key principles is that the best way to build wealth is not to lose it. So, what does that mean, exactly?

Far too often, people looking to build wealth have the expectation that investing needs to be complex and sophisticated in order to make real money. For many, investing is an "ego patting" exercise that gives you something to talk to your friends about at the pub on a Saturday night. Nothing is more exciting than talking about the "Blockchain Long-Short Global Growth" hedge fund that can only be accessed by the elite few. But more often than not, the sexier the investment, the higher the risk.

Warren Buffett has built his career on being able to choose the best boring companies in the world that he knows follow a tried-and-true plan to achieve their profit and growth targets. While everyone else is looking for the next Facebook, Warren is reviewing long-established companies that have track history he can count on so that he may make an informed decision that doesn't lose him money. By avoiding losses that can come from having a volatile and unpredictable investment, you have control over your asset base with the intention of achieving consistent forward momentum from capital growth.

Let's look at an example.

Assume that you had $100,000 to invest and you bought shares in an investment in Joe Blow's hedge fund at $1 each. You now have 100,000 shares in the fund. Over the next twelve months, the fund falls by 10 percent, and your total investment value is now $90,000.

How much do you need to make to get your $100,000 back? Well, 10 percent only gets you back to $99,000, so you need to make closer to 12 percent just to break even again.

As you can see, a loss, especially in the initial stages of investing, can be damaging and take time for your portfolio to recover from. Unfortunately, most of us don't have the experience of Warren Buffett to know what companies to buy and when to buy them. With this being said, I have spent my career trying to help my clients steer clear from heavy losses from high-risk investments and have the right wealth protection strategies in place to set them up for a successful wealth journey.

Remember, every part of your wealth plan should tick our three self-assessment questions, which are as follows:

1. Is it simple?

2. Is it sustainable?

3. Is it scalable?

When you are applying this to wealth protection, there is a straightforward process to follow to ensure you cover your bases. The aim of this is to ensure that you are able to understand your objectives before you dive into building your wealth. Your plan should be to always ensure that what you have now is safe and secure (we will define this more later) before you dive into the next stage of your wealth journey.

So how do we do this? We define what we are trying to achieve.

When we invest, we need to understand what we are working toward. Investing is a vehicle that ultimately gets us to a goal some point in the future. What many people fail to do is clearly define their goal of what investing aims to help them achieve. As such, many take too much risk or not enough to give them the highest probability of reaching their destination.

Let's say, for example, that you want to save for a property deposit for which you aim to have $100,000 in ten years' time. We have now defined the final amount and the timeframe we have to work with, allowing us to work out how much risk or contribution we need to make to the investment to get us to where we want to go. It is important to have as much clarity around the goal as possible. For most of us, the goal is either a capital goal, such as a sum of money we need to fulfil a purchase we want to make, or an income goal, such as an income we ideally want to receive passively from our portfolio at some point in the future.

## Clarity Is the Key

I have seen so many clients who have ambitions to create as much wealth as possible, whether that be ten properties or $5,000,000 in assets, but not many take the time to ask themselves why. Is the plan to have the ability to not have to work anymore from the income you receive from rent? Or is the plan to have a sufficient amount of money to allow you to buy your dream home? Defining the destination not only makes selecting the most appropriate investment easier, it also helps us stay the course of sacrifice in the process of working toward the destination.

It is up to you to define the destination, as this is all about what you want. To make life easy, we have created a compounding calculator that allows you to plug in a future goal of either income or capital, the timeframe you want to wait, the amount you want to contribute, and the expected return. This will act as a guide to point you in the right direction, but it is important to note that this isn't an exact science.

If you want to get a better understanding of what you need to do to get to your destination, please get in touch with us.

# CHAPTER 7

# Embarking on Your Trip: Wealth Creation

Wealth creation is the reason most of you purchased this book, and to be honest, it is what a lot of wealth commentators talk about as their primary subject matter. I don't disagree with the importance of a well-thought-out investment strategy, but I have seen that the real value in financial planning isn't really investment related. As we discussed in the previous chapter, wealth creation is more about wealth protection than anything else. And in my experience, I have seen that some of the most successful people focus on two key strategies as a means to build their wealth: (1) creating their own business or (2) buying good-quality assets that have consistent performance and allow compounding to do the rest.

My guide to wealth creation is insanely simple. I will give you my rulebook for investing, which I use for my own portfolio and for advising my clients. It has allowed me to help them accumulate over $1 billion in total wealth. The next thing I want to give you is a crash course on how to avoid making bad decisions, which will lead you further from your goals and which have resulted in countless others ruining themselves financially due to straying down a dangerous path.

It is a dangerous world out there in the financial services industry, and there are endless amounts of peddlers trying to make a quick buck from you if you aren't careful. I find myself frequently talking my clients out of making bad decisions, because there are some really compelling offers out there at face value that can be extremely detrimental to your wealth plan. It seems that more often than not, everyone is looking for a get-rich-quick scheme, expecting that a single decision will ultimately lead to a life of financial abundance. If this were true, there would be more rich people in the world.

The following is our guide to wealth creation:

1.  Define your destination.

2.  Set a reasonable timeframe.

3.  Understand your attitude toward risk.

4.  Educate yourself, and set realistic expectations.

5.  If it sounds too good to be true, it usually is.

6.  Diversify.

7.  Contribute consistently.

8.  Don't watch the news.

9.  Stick the course.

Avoid the following:

1.  Hedge funds with high fees.

2.  Sophisticated investments that you don't understand—options, CFDs, futures.

3.  Too much leverage.

4.  Keeping all your eggs in one basket.

5.  Always chasing the winners.

6. Anyone promising you a positive return.

7. Gambling with money you can't afford to lose.

## Define Your Destination

Ok, Jackson, we get the idea! You keep telling us about this destination over and over again. Well, that's how important it is. Far too often, people see being wealthy as the destination itself, and unfortunately, it's not. Your wealth is not the goal. Your wealth is just another vehicle in your financial world that gives you the freedom to have more choices. Wealth expands life's menu and gives you the ability to choose an appetizer, main, and dessert.

The question is, how much wealth do you really need to get what you want?

In my experience, most people's financial goals can be summed up in a pretty short list:

1. Buy a nice house.

2. Live a good lifestyle

3. Provide for the family.

4. Send the kids to a good school or give them a head start.

5. Have a nice holiday.

6. Build enough wealth to be able to choose whether to work.

7. Give back to family, friends, and so on.

8. Leave a legacy.

## Set a Reasonable Timeframe

There's a saying I use a lot, and it holds true almost daily in my business working with my clients:

"Most people overestimate what they can do in a year and underestimate what they can do in ten."

For some reason, most of us need to have everything now. And for most, anything that takes longer than a year or two is too far away to even think about right now. Impatience seems to be getting worse with each generation. I continue to see Generation Y people complaining about property prices and being unable to afford a deposit while they spend every last dollar on their morning goji berry chai latte and smashed avocado on toast. Hard life, right?

I was guilty of this myself, and I personally lost quite a bit of money having a crack at a get-rich-quick scheme when I first started my career as an adviser. I was working for a big financial services company, and I was working as a phone-based adviser with a team of around fifteen other guys. One member of our group started trading contracts for difference, or CFDs, which are basically a form of financial market gambling. The premise is that you find a stock, currency, or commodity, and you make a bet that the investment will either go up or down. Sounds simple, right? I thought so too!

The risk with CFDs is that you don't own the physical asset, whether that be the shares or the gold you are trading. This means that you have no security to hold onto. The reason you can make a huge return on your investment is that your money is leveraged, meaning you increase the potential for return and, conversely, increase your risk. Unlike with shares, if the market falls, you can always hold your stocks until the market recovers. With CFDs, there can be unlimited losses in some instances, which can be very dangerous.

My teammates and I started trading, and over a number of months, I had a 1,000 percent return on investment. I was bragging about it, thinking I was some master trader that had somehow worked the market out, and I was planning on how I would ride the wave all the way to financial freedom. Coincidentally, I received a call from a guy looking to get some advice, and after having a conversation for a while, he started telling me his story.

"So, I used to be a trader . . . I did pretty well with it for a while there," he said, with the sound of disappointment in his voice.

"Oh, yeah? I do a bit of trading myself for fun," I responded confidently, oblivious of the undertone in his voice. There was a silence that caught my attention.

"You said you used to be a trader. What happened?" I asked him inquisitively.

"Well, I was working for an investment bank doing well and discovered CFDs. I started trading and making some good money, and when I thought I had figured it all out . . ." I listened intently, as I was really curious at this point.

"I mortgaged my house and borrowed money from my best friend and pumped it all into my trading account, so I could take more aggressive positions. I was doing well for a while, and all of a sudden something went wrong, and I lost it all." He continued as I kept quiet.

"I couldn't pay my mortgage, so the bank took my house. My wife left me, and I lost my best mate. I have just tried to avoid going bankrupt and get back on my feet. . ."

I remember the call as if it were yesterday. But unfortunately, I didn't learn my lesson from his firsthand experience. We all kept trading, and as we progressed, we took more and more risk to try and amplify our success, with no regard for what we were doing. It was December, and we had all been called into a meeting. All of a sudden, our mobile phones started going off. One after one, we pulled them out to check what was going on, and as I looked around the room, all I saw was fear on everyone's face. I checked my phone, and the worst had happened. The market suffered a flash crash, and as my active trades started to fall, there was nothing I could do to stop it except watch and hope the market stopped plummeting.

In a matter of a few minutes, my account and my colleagues' accounts went all the way to zero. In total, we collectively lost around $100,000. That doesn't seem like a huge sum of money, but for twenty-year-old advisers who thought we knew it all, it was a lot.

So, what did I learn from the experience? I learned that you shouldn't invest in anything you don't understand. I learned that without ownership of an asset, you have no security. I also learned that gambling is dangerous, regardless of whether it is in the casino or in the financial markets.

## Understand Your Attitude Toward Risk

Risk is a funny thing because it is very subjective. Some people think skydiving is completely safe but refuse to ride a motorbike in case they have an accident. Some will only own property, because they are terrified of the share market. In my experience, it all comes down to education. I'm sure all of you have heard some story about a friend of a friend who lost everything after the share market crashed, but the fact is that there is likely more to the story than meets the eye. When it comes to investments, it is all about risk versus return. Once we have considered our destination and how long we are prepared to wait to reach the destination, the risk we take should be just enough to give us some level of certainty around the probability of achieving the outcome in our desired timeframe.

I want to help educate you about the relationship of risk versus return when it comes to each primary asset class in Australia. These classes consist of cash, fixed interest and bonds, property, Australian shares, and international shares. Each asset class has a suggested investment timeframe that gives us a guide for how long we will have to wait to weather any potential storm that presents itself along the way.

It was Warren Buffet that once said, "we pay a big price for certainty," and I totally agree. If you want certainty when it comes to investments, you are best to stick all of your money in the bank. The only certainty you will have if you do that is that your money won't do much and that you will be lucky to keep up with inflation after tax.

Let's get into the history behind each asset class in order to give you some insight around what has happened over time. Keep in mind that historical performance is not an indicator of future performance. All it does is help us set some expectations of what we could expect into the future. It is also important to remember that inflation is our biggest enemy when we consider investing. We need to ensure that after tax, our investment is above inflation, because if we are unable to keep up with inflation, the value of our money will start going backward. As of my writing this book, the current inflation rate in Australia is 1.9 percent, but it is expected to remain between 2.5 percent and 3 percent on average.

## Cash

Cash includes savings accounts and term deposits and is a staple in most Australians' personal banking. With easy access, simple online applications, and ability to transfer between accounts quickly, cash can be an easy way to save but also very tempting and easy to "borrow" from.

**Timeframe**—Less than one year.

**Pros**—Cash is safe and secure, government guaranteed, and it can be accessed immediately.

**Cons**—Cash brings low returns given low interest rates, and it doesn't increase in capital value.

Fixed Interest and Bonds.

Fixed interest and bonds are loans from you, the investor, to a government or corporation in exchange for a rate of return relative to the current interest rate and the risk associated with the company itself. This risk is associated to its credit rating and will adjust the interest you are likely to receive. Bonds also carry a duration for investment (one, three, five, ten-plus years), and the longer the bond duration, the larger the effect interest rates can have on the value of your bond. In short, bonds are riskier than cash but less risky than shares if you invest in governments and corporations with good credit ratings.

**Timeframe**—One to three years.

**Pros**—These have a higher rate of return than cash. They can be invested in large governments and corporations.

**Cons**—Some bonds can be very high risk depending on their credit rating. Interest rates present a substantial risk to bond values.

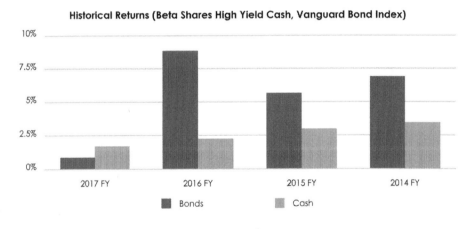

Figure 8

## Infrastructure and Listed Property

Infrastructure is an investment into companies that provide services, such as utilities, water piping, airports, highways, toll roads, and many others. Infrastructure generally has long-term, fixed contracts in place with high barriers to entry for competition, so infrastructure assets generally experience less volatility than shares and pay high income.

Listed property normally includes trusts that own commercial real estate, such as Westfield, Scentre Group, and Stockland. These property trusts provide exposure to the growth in the commercial property market while giving you diversification across multiple properties within the one fund. Listed property has experienced substantial volatility. In some cases, it has experienced more volatility than the stock market.

**Timeframe**—Five to seven years plus.

**Pros**—Infrastructure provides some consistency while having growth potential and income returns. Listed property provides more diversification than owning a single property does.

**Cons**—Both are classed as growth assets and can experience volatility over the short to medium term.

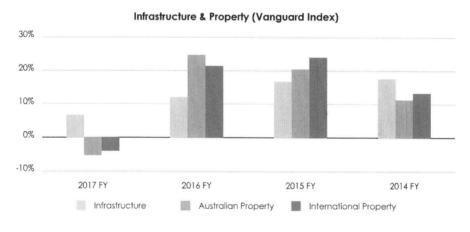

Figure 9

## Australian Shares

Shares are partial ownership in a company listed on the stock market. When you own shares, you will experience the outcomes of what that company does and how it performs along with how the overall market performs. In turn, you will experience the outcome of how the market perceives the value of that company, which affects the value of the shares. Many companies also pay dividends, which is a distribution of the profit to shareholders.

**Timeframe**—7 years plus

**Pros**—You are able to own a piece of a company, shares have outperformed cash over the long term, there are tax advantages of making profits from shares, including capital gains tax discounts and franking credits.

**Cons**—The share market can be volatile. And even though a company might be performing well, this doesn't always translate to the share price increasing.

## International Shares

As with Australian shares, international shares are partial ownership in a multinational company located outside of Australia, including those in the US, UK, and EU. Given the size of these companies, they generally experience different growth characteristics than the Australian market but still experience volatility.

**Timeframe**—7 years plus

**Pros**—You are able to own a piece of a large multinational company; international shares have outperformed Australian shares and cash over the long term.

**Cons**—As it is a growth asset, it can experience volatility, and in the global financial crisis, the international share market experienced over a 50 percent fall in overall value.

## Emerging Markets

Emerging markets refers to investing in smaller countries such as Thailand, Brazil, Russia, India, and China. Just like with international and Australian shares, you are owning a piece of a company in an emerging country. But these countries generally experience higher growth, higher volatility, and some additional geo-political risk, which can increase volatility.

**Timeframe**—Seven to ten years plus

**Pros**—Emerging markets such as China have experienced substantial growth, especially with companies such as Alibaba, which has resulted in substantial capital growth.

**Cons**—With any investment that experiences high returns there is also high risk, and these generally experience more volatility than those in established markets.

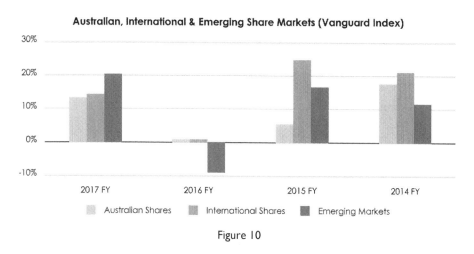

Figure 10

## Australian Residential Property

Australians love property, and we breathe bricks and mortar. I am sure you have heard how everyone you know has made a killing with direct property, and in some areas of Australia, property has done extremely well. It is also important to consider that due to direct property not being regulated by a stock exchange or providing investors with access to data that could drive a decision, property involves a lot of sentiment and emotion, which can also drive the price.

**Timeframe**—Seven years plus

**Pros**—This has historically been a stable investment in metropolitan areas across Australia, allows for high levels of leverage, which can increase return on investment.

**Cons**—This is illiquid, which means you cannot sell the asset quickly or with minimal costs. Also, like the share market, this lacks the level of transparency around "fair value," it and can be driven substantially by emotion, which can inflate or deflate the price.

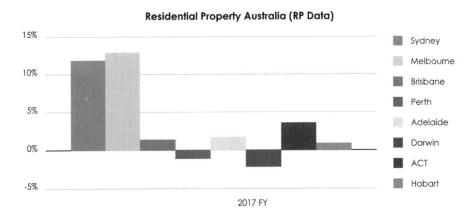

Figure 11

So, with all of this data around pros, cons, and historical returns, what the hell do we do next? Should we chase the investment that has done the best and hope it will do the same? Unfortunately, it isn't that easy. I have always found it best to diversify, put my eggs into multiple baskets, and let the market take care of the rest. This is what I have always recommended to my clients and used for my own wealth creation, and this ensures I have enough time available to do the things I really enjoy.

But Jackson, aren't there sexier ways to make lots of money?

Well, yes, there are plenty of sexy ways to try and make money, but most result in underperformance, excessive risks, and net returns that are far below the market average, especially once tax has been taken into account. A survey was done by DALBAR, an American investment research company, regarding the average return of a retail investor in the US. It was found that the US market returned on average 10.28 percent per year since 1985–2015. In comparison, the average investor only made 3.66 percent! Let's assume that you invested $10,000 in 1985 and forgot about it until today. You would have $252,576 if you earned 10.28 percent per annum and only $32,746 if you earned 3.66 percent, which is a huge difference of almost $220,000! If that doesn't convince you of the importance of diversification, I don't know what will.

So how do you get this diversification? Well, the easiest way is through index investing.

An index is all of the companies that exist in a particular market. For example, the ASX index is composed of the top three hundred companies in Australia. The index gives you the average rate of return achieved by all of the companies within that index based on their size relative to the other companies in that index.

Index investing is the process of buying an investment fund that provides you with complete access to a particular investment index. In turn, this gives you access to huge diversification at a low price. Most index funds charge as little as 0.1 percent per annum as a fee and provide benefits such as the following:

1. High levels of liquidity, so you can sell out quickly
2. Tax-effectiveness, as investments within the index are rarely sold
3. Access to hundreds of companies in one place
4. Little maintenance required from the investor
5. Access with as little as $1,000

# Educate Yourself and Set Realistic Expectations

"Educate yourself and set realistic expectations" is a saying I use all too often, as it seems that most people whom I speak with tend to have unrealistic expectations about what they are trying to achieve. It is almost as if they want to set the bar so unbelievably high so as to justify why they never achieve what they aim for.

"Formal education will make you a living. Self-education will make you a fortune"- Jim Rohn

I recently met with a potential client who was looking to get some advice about her wealth planning. In our initial discussions, I asked her what the main reason was for her contacting me, to which she quickly replied,

"I am looking for someone who is willing to help me create $500,000 a year of passive income. Unless you can help me with this, I won't work with you."

I pondered for a moment and responded, "Fair enough. Well, how did you come up with that number?"

Once again, without even thinking twice, she replied, "That's just what I want."

After taking some time to speak with her, I learned that her household income was $150,000. She had a mortgage of around $650,000 and two young kids. Her main goal was to pay off her home loan and work toward being in a position that allowed her to choose whether she had to work. She also wanted to give her kids a nest egg to help them get into the property market. When we actually did the math, assuming she paid off her home and her kids had become self-sufficient, her desired lifestyle cost was only around $80,000 a year.

What does this example teach us?

Well, it teaches us a number of things. First, it shows us that many people are driven by blind ambition. They are working from preconceived ideas of what financial freedom actually means without understanding what their idea of financial freedom is. Second, after setting reasonable expectations that were linked to her own situation, she was able to have a plan linked to more than just a number. It was linked to tangible outcomes that the numbers were calculated from that included paying off her debt, helping her kids, and living the lifestyle she wanted. Third, it created a certain level of accountability because now the goals were real, measurable, and completely reliant on her ability to follow the path.

Education is not just about understanding the different investment options, but it also about educating yourself around what you really want in life. As humans, we are constantly prioritizing what we do with our available resources, whether they be time or money. At the end of the day, these are the only two commodities we have, and it is a matter of working out how you trade one for the other.

We have talked a lot about goals throughout this book, and this is for good reason. I want to help you create the habit of taking the time to consider what you really want and create a hierarchy of goals linked to your day-to-day life. An important exercise to consider around this is based on a theory called Maslow's hierarchy of needs. In Maslow's theory, he talks about the need for individuals to achieve a certain level of acceptance for each level of their needs before they can consider progressing to the next. An example of this is that you cannot start working toward buying an investment property if you do not have food to eat.

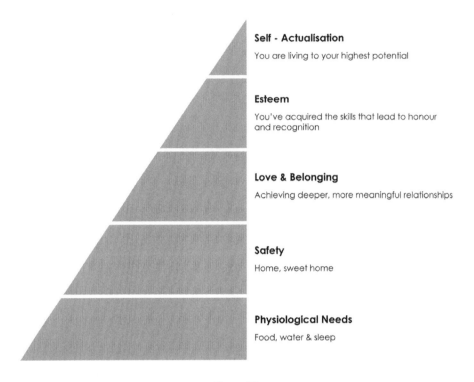

**Self - Actualisation**
You are living to your highest potential

**Esteem**
You've acquired the skills that lead to honour and recognition

**Love & Belonging**
Achieving deeper, more meaningful relationships

**Safety**
Home, sweet home

**Physiological Needs**
Food, water & sleep

Figure 12

When it comes to educating yourself about your needs, it is important to consider where you are in the above pyramid (see figure 12) and prioritize your goals based on the things that are important at either your current level or the one above. For example, if you don't own your home and you haven't started saving for a deposit, this should be your primary goal to achieve your safety needs.

Once you are content with your goals education, it is now time to have a better understanding of what you choose to invest in. I have always followed the motto "Stick to what you know. Outsource everything else." And this regards investment selection as well. In addition to the last topic, even if we choose to invest in low-cost index funds, there is still a process of how you choose to allocate your money to them. This is why we have developed a number of innovative solutions to help investors, ranging from first-time investors to seasoned experts, to access a well-thought-out portfolio based on their risk profile and goals.

To find out more information about this, please check out our module on the portal for

# If It Sounds Too Good to Be True, It Usually Is

The world of investments is a scary, crazy place. And investors are easy prey for sharks, who are circling constantly, waiting for their next target. We all want to believe that there is some get-rich scheme out there that will answer all of our problems and set us up for life. This is just like our wishing that Santa Claus were real or that we actually had a serious chance at winning the lottery. Unfortunately, this is all make-believe, with slim odds of success.

This is the driving force that leads most to make poor financial and investment decisions. We want to believe that what we hear is true. We ignore all of the warning signs that should make us run for the hills.

When I was around twenty years old, I had been saving for a while in an effort to buy my first property. I was always ambitious, and I always wanted to be the first or the youngest to achieve certain goals in life, so I dedicated myself entirely to trying to save to get into the property market. I went to investment seminars, home shows, and property education groups and tried to learn as much as I could to get ahead. At a home show in Sydney, I was given a DVD about a woman who was teaching how to make millions in profits using property without even making a deposit. Sounds amazing, right?

Well, I took the DVD home and watched it intently. She was very professional and engaging, and she said all of the right things. She asked rhetorical questions like "Are you frustrated that you aren't getting ahead fast enough? Are you wanting to live life on your terms and make money work for you?"

Well, of course I did! I was a twenty-year-old kid wanting to reach my goals and break free from the chains that had for decades impeded my parents from getting ahead.

As she went on, she very quickly shifted into selling a program about how to become a property developer and make money from the bank without having to put down a dollar. She spoke very directly to the point of how it worked, how she had made millions, and how she had helped countless others make millions too. It seemed perfect, and I enrolled in her next seminar, which was the following week in the city.

The room was packed to the brim with people. I would safely say there were over two hundred attendees at this event who were all sitting with the same look on their face as if they were waiting to be told all of the answers to every question they had ever pondered. The presenter came out and recycled verbatim exactly what she had said on the DVD. It seemed I was the only one not hooked into a trance-like state, as I felt something wasn't quite right.

As her presentation came to a close, she directed everyone to go to the back of the room and enrol in her intensive program, which she promised would teach all of the tricks of the development trade, mentor everyone to get started, and ensure they were able to achieve financial freedom and abundance—all in exchange for tens of thousands in fees! I saw 75 percent of the people in the room run to the back to register, willing to put their hard-earned savings on the line to have a gamble at what she had to offer. I, however, wasn't yet convinced.

I went home, and I thought to myself, "If this woman backs herself so much, I need her to tell me herself that I should go ahead with her course." Sounds fair, right? Well, it was a big roll of the dice in hindsight.

I sent her an email via her website that went something like this:

ATTN CEO: I need your help

Dear *Insert name here*

I attended your seminar last night in Sydney, and I need your advice. I have been saving for two years to build up a deposit to buy my first property, and I am nearly ready to do so. I want to get ahead, but I need to know I am making the right decision. I need to choose whether to keep doing what I am doing or whether I should use my money for my deposit on your course.

Can you advise me what you would do in my position and if you really think I would be better off investing my money into what you can teach me?

I look forward to hearing from you.

Jackson

So, I waited and waited, and no response. Probably a blessing in disguise, right? I went on with my life and didn't buy the course, but I always had the thought of "What if?" in my mind. Many years later, I was reading the paper, and what did I see? The CEO of this company had been charged for misleading information, the company went into liquidation, and she was unable to run a company again. I remember having a sigh of relief, but it was quickly followed by concern for all of those who weren't so lucky. What had to happen to them in order to force the authorities to hold her accountable for her actions? Did they lose just their thousands for the course, or did they lose everything?

The reason I tell you this story is that when it sounds too good to be true, it usually is. There is no such thing as a guaranteed return, a risk-free investment, or a once-in-a-lifetime opportunity. Sometimes the most boring investments can be the best ones because they are tried and true and allow you to take calculated risks.

# Diversify

Have you ever heard the saying "don't put all of your eggs in one basket"? I'm sure you have—far too many times. Diversification is really about having options, depending on the timeline before you reach your goals or objectives. The aim of diversification is spreading your risk into multiple asset classes and should be based on your tolerance to risk or volatility and your goals and objectives.

# Contribute Consistently

One of the objections I hear most when it comes to investing in growth assets like shares is "What if the market crashes tomorrow?" This is always my favourite question, as I see how people change their opinions over time with the right perspective. The market is volatile. We know that on average, there is some kind of market correction one out of every four or five years that results in a negative return. But what happens in the other years? Well, historically the market has always gone up.

So, with that being said, why don't we just wait until the market crashes to put our money in? It isn't that easy. There have been very smart people trying to time the market for decades with no success, and time after time, these people have lost lots of money. What history has shown is that markets are unpredictable over the short term, but over the long term, everything works out.

Now, I know this is fantastic in theory, but when you invest $500,000 and the market falls 20 percent, that can be pretty nerve-racking. So, what do you do about it? Let me give you an example.

Let's assume you went shopping and bought one kilogram of oranges for $2. The next day you went back and saw that oranges were on sale for $1. What would you do? Well, given the small scale of the loss, it probably wouldn't bother you. But in reality, this is a 50 percent loss on your investment so how does that make you feel?

On the flip side, if you didn't buy the oranges today and returned to the store the next day and saw that they were $1, what would you do?

Would you consider buying double the amount for the same price as the previous day knowing that you just got an amazing deal?

Given that you are likely buying oranges because you like to make fresh juice, the price is unlikely to influence your decision too much. But what if this were your business and you made a living buying and selling oranges? It is likely that your perspective would change. If you bought oranges yesterday at $2 and today you realize you can get them for half the price, I am sure you might be pretty annoyed. You might consider increasing your prices, but this might take you longer to sell them to make a profit, so what else can you do?

In this situation you can implement a strategy known as *dollar cost averaging*, which means you buy more oranges irrespective of the price on a regular and recurring basis, so over time the purchase price averages out. For example, if you buy one kilogram at $2 and one kilogram at $1, your average price per kilogram is now $1.50. The same goes for any unitized investment, such as shares.

The idea is to contribute every single month, regardless of what happens. Over time we will capture the highs and the lows, and it will average out to maximize your investment while spreading the risk of timing the market.

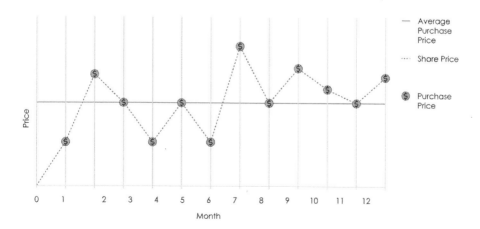

Figure 13

This strategy also helps with investor psychology because it helps you overcome the fear of the ups and downs and helps you stick the course. Remember, trying to time the market is a mugs game, so stick to tried-and-true strategies that have worked for generations.

## Don't Watch the News

When was the last time you watched the news and saw something that evoked positive emotions from you? I know that for me, these experiences are few and far between. The news profits primarily from two key drivers; fear and greed, and the one they use most often is fear as it resonates with everyone, regardless of financial position.

With this in mind, modern day journalism loves a good scary story as they know it creates viral content, results in more watchers or readers and in turn, generates them more revenue. The news is a well-oiled machine and runs off fear mongering. The news serves an important role to keep us informed but when it comes to driving financial decisions, the news is not your friend.

It is true that news can drive investment markets and there have been substantial market movements as a result of publicized information spreading like wildfire. This has been the case with the constant publicity of the Australian property market and the so-called "Property Bubble" which has been featured more than any other investment news for the last year or so. With this being said, it is the media's agenda to spread popular content that evokes emotion. When you see something on the news, it is likely one or both of the following;

1.  Biased short-term opinions.

2.  Old news that is out dated.

With this in mind, it is best to steer clear of popular media sources when making objective financial decisions. Take advice from credible sources of current information and link this information back to your own personal goals before making a knee-jerk decision. Remember, if we all listened to the news we would probably spend our life locked inside in fear of the 'what if'!

## Stick the Course

One of the common mistakes of many amateur investors is constantly trying to make changes and 'optimize' their strategy thinking doing more is better. More often than not, doing less is more and knowing that good things take time. Once you have decided on a course of action it is important to continue to repeat that action for enough time for it to work its magic for you.

The temptation to change what you are doing is real as there is always that little voice in the back of your head that tells you what you are doing isn't right and you need to do more. I have found that the seed of doubt is greatest when you are either unsure of whether the action you have taken is the right one or if you are unsure of what your actions are leading you towards.

I remember as a kid my father used to take me fishing at a local lagoon. I was always an impatient kid and sitting around waiting for a fish to bite was torture for me. I always loved fishing with my dad, but he was constantly lecturing me for not taking enough time between casting my line out and bringing it back in to check on it. After casting my bait into the water, I would wait for a few minutes before the voice came back.

"I bet you didn't cast into the right area where the fish are, I bet the bait has fallen off already, maybe you should cast into that dark spot over there."

Before long I would be reeling my line back in succumbing to the seed of doubt.

"Jack! You need to be patient. Trust you have done the right thing and leave your line in the water. Fishing is a waiting game so just watch and wait." My dad said over and over again.

After a while I would sigh and listen to him, fighting the urge to reel in my line. After ten minutes or so, BANG! I would always get a bite.

The moral to this is that you need to get clear on your objectives, so you can better manage your emotions along the journey. If you are clear on what you are trying to achieve, for example, you want to catch a fish for dinner, you will then be able to question your decisions when working towards that goal. Additionally, you need to trust in your decisions long enough to allow them to yield results for you and leave your line in the water long enough to see if the fish will bite before checking your hook or trying a new area to land a bite.

When you choose to take action, stick the path and keep acting consistently in pursuit of your goals and believe what you are doing is right.

## Areas to avoid;
## Hedge funds with high fees

I am sure that most of you have heard of hedge funds but for those of you who haven't I will give you two definitions; the one their sales and marketing team tells you and the real definition.

## Their definition

A hedge fund is an actively managed portfolio for investors wanting to out-perform the market and experience less ups and downs due to market volatility. The fund managers will use their expertise and skill to pick the right investments at the right time along with being able to implement sophisticated strategies that maximize returns for their investors.

Sounds great right?

## The definition they don't want to know

A hedge fund is an actively managed portfolio that promises to beat the market over the long term by using overly-complex strategies aimed to confuse the investor and validate the value of the fund managers skills along with create a reliance on the investor to continue to use the fund manager for the long term. In truth, most hedge funds under-perform the benchmark and charge fees upwards of 2% per annum plus performance fees if they make a positive return.

Not so sexy now?

Over the last few decades, we have seen a rise in actively managed funds who spend tremendous amounts on their marketing and sales budgets in order to attract uneducated investors to buy into their products. To put this all into perspective, many studies have found that the average return of many hedge fund investors has been as little as 2% per annum after fees and taxes which is a scary thought!

To further illustrate this point, our friend Warren Buffett saw this coming over a decade ago. In 2007 he made a $2 million bet with a hedge fund manager Ted Seides who was surprisingly the only fund manager willing to wager their skills against the market. The wager stated that the hedge fund manager would be unable to out-perform the S&P500 index over a ten-year period.

The hedge fund manager admitted defeat in May 2017 after only increasing his initial $1 million investment to $1.22 million compared to the $1.85 million Buffett was able to build by acquiring the S&P500 index.

Need I say more?

## Sophisticated investments you don't understand- options, CFDs, Futures & Cryptocurrency

Much like hedge funds, the idea of sophisticated investments is really exciting, and the temptation is sometimes hard to resist, even for seasoned professionals like myself. There is always something new and exciting on the horizon when it comes to investment opportunities, whether that be a new disruptive tech start-up, a peer to peer lending platform or the latest craze of cryptocurrency and bitcoin. The common theme with a lot of these things is that they are often overhyped by popular media outlets, driven up in value by 'pack mentality investors' and often correct or fall aggressively when these investors get spooked and try to cash in.

There is definitely a place in the world for sophisticated and speculative investment opportunities and I can't argue with the fact that many people have become incredibly wealthy as a result of taking a punt, but it is important to consider the risks, particularly when you are just getting started on your wealth journey or haven't established a solid base yet.

Over the last few months I have been asked countless times from my clients and personal network what I think of this whole cryptocurrency craze and my answer is simple- only invest in what you understand otherwise you are just gambling, and much like gambling you should only put in what you can afford to lose. To further illustrate, as of writing this book Bitcoin has gone from around $1,000 USD in January 2017 to a high of $19,000 USD in December 2017 only to fall again to around $12,000 before 2017 came to an end. This level of volatility is scary and illustrates the level of risk associated with these types of investments.

When it comes to investing, there are some simple rules you need to ask yourself. If you answer no to any of them, you should seriously consider not investing as it is likely a gamble and you should be prepared to wave your money goodbye.

1. Do you understand the investment?
2. Does the investment have real worth? (physical asset, proven track record, produces income, tangible value)
3. Does the investment have a track history of more than 10 years?

4.  Do you understand the risks associated with the investment?

5.  Are you confident that the investment will help you achieve your goals?

Ask yourself these questions honestly and objectively before diving in feet first. As discussed in our wealth pyramid section of the book, you need to ensure you are accumulating wealth in the right order and looking at ways to take the least amount of risk to achieve the outcomes you want in life. Don't be driven just by the potential for returns, consider what you might lose in the process.

## Be careful of leverage- magnification of risk

Leverage is a great tool for building wealth as discussed in the foundations, but it can be a very dangerous one if not used appropriately. For many Australians, borrowing to invest, particularly in property has been a strategy used by many for generations with fantastic results due to the outstanding performance of most property markets in most metropolitan areas of Australia. As such, this has led to many of us become desensitized to the risks associated with having too much debt especially when things don't go to plan.

When it comes to debt, we need to always be wary of what could happen, and we need to be considerate of the fact that property markets may not always give us the returns we hope for.

As we discussed in the debt part of the foundations, paying down debts is a risk-free return as the interest we avoid paying is equal to the equivalent investment return. We need to consider the same in reverse as the banks will always come knocking for their repayment, even if times get tough and you can't afford to pay them.

I have seen far too often an investor over-extend themselves to buy an investment property and scrape by each month thinking they are doing the right thing by pushing it to the limit. Only to have a property vacant for 3 months and end up racking up credit card debts and personal loans trying to keep the property afloat. Your wealth journey is difficult enough as it is so be careful with how you utilize debt to achieve your goals.

## Don't keep all your eggs in one basket

Another common mistake is that a lot of investors find a strategy that works and only put money into that one place over and over again- we will talk about this more in the Wealth Management part of the book. Remember, one investment might yield fantastic returns if you have all of your money in it, but what if the opposite was true? What if the investment fell by 50% overnight and what would that do to your future planning?

Diversification is the key to passive investment and it aims to ensure we don't keep all of our money in the same place, in the same kinds of assets which all move in the same direction at the same time. There is such a thing as over-diversification, but it is a good idea to have a solid mix of cash, bonds, shares and property to give yourself a well-rounded portfolio and minimize the risk of flash crashes that affect a particular sector of the investment market.

## Don't always chase the winners

We have all been in a situation where we have been told by a family member or a friend of an investment opportunity they have made a killing from. That particular stock or suburb that gave them a 3x return on investment that they preach at every barbeque. It is always tempting but more often than not, the pack mentality of chasing the winners rarely pays off.

In my previous example of the Global Financial Crisis, it was common place for markets to return 20% per annum and at this time people got greedy. We are seeing this now in the Sydney and Melbourne property markets where people have experienced huge returns and the old FOMO kicks in for anyone who has sat on the fence- Fear Of Missing Out.

We are inspired by pack mentality and I can admit that I have been tempted to follow the pack myself chasing investment trends but my experience and understanding of markets helps me to navigate the storm with certainty. As the old saying goes "What goes up, must come down" and the highest performing stock, managed fund or suburb in any one year is rarely ever the best the following year.

Don't fall into the trap of constantly trying to chase the best performer every single year as you run the risk of doing more damage than good. When looking for investments, you want to look for something that has experienced consistent performance and hasn't suffered from the boom and bust style volatility that many of these 'winning investments' tend to have. Consistency is key and there is no point punting on something that has already gone up 400% unless there is a way to justify it continuing to do so through the demonstration of real intrinsic value, not just investor speculation driving up the price.

## Avoid anyone promising you a positive return

The world is full of spruikers and unfortunately, they aren't going anywhere anytime soon. Given the world of money and investing is so complex, there have been thousands of crooks who have made careers from taking advantage of everyday people like you and I. It is important to understand that no investment return is guaranteed and for any expected return there is normally the comparable level of risk to go with it.

Think about it, if you had a friend who approached you for a loan which they would use to fund a business deal and offered to pay you a 20% rate of return for lending them $50,000 for 12 months it might sound like a pretty good deal right? Firstly, we need to consider the 'why' before diving in

- Why is he paying such a high return?

- Why is he not going to a cheaper lender to finance this loan? Eg a bank will offer a personal loan at around 13%

The motivating factors would likely be that a) they are able to generate a substantially higher return than 20% to make the payment to you worthwhile or b) they aren't able to get the money elsewhere and they don't want to lose the opportunity.

In any case, there are risks and for the return they need to be considered carefully. There is a chance your friend might default on the loan as the business deal didn't go to plan and as a result, you get nothing in return. Pretty scary right?

The same goes for guaranteed returns- there is really no such thing. Once again, you pay a big price for certainty and you should always question the risks of your decision before you commit to an investment. My mantra has always been, if you are being promised a return you should run from the hills.

An example of this was a recent email I received from a so called 'property advisory firm'. They were offering investment properties in the centre of Brisbane with rental guarantees with a 5% yield. I immediately thought, "if this was a well desired property that people wanted to live in, why would you need a rental guarantee?"

My thoughts were correct.

As it stands right now, Brisbane CBD has a vacancy rate of 6.9% compared to the rest of the country at 2.4%. That is a huge difference and indicates a substantial over-supply of property. This is the reason they are offering a guarantee as it is the only way an investor would buy the property.

Moral of the story, ensure you ask the right questions around the risks and do your research!

## Don't gamble with money you can't afford to lose

Let's face it, most of us have had a punt on something at some point of our life. Whether that be a slap on the pokies, the horses or a speculative investment that we heard about from a mate. There are always going to be opportunities that come up along the way that will catch our attention and leave us wanting to find out more. The most important thing is to separate the idea of investing and gambling when it comes to assessing these opportunities.

An investment is something you understand, that has a track history of performance that aligns with your objectives and that has real intrinsic value such as metropolitan property or blue-chip shares and index funds.

A gamble is something you don't really understand, haven't likely done before or done often, has no real consistent track history and has huge potential and huge potential for loss also. When it comes to gambling, you should only put in what you can afford to lose and that won't break the bank or send you miles off track for your goals as a result of things not going to plan.

Be careful with your gambling as regardless of whether it is traditional gambling like poker or going to the race track, gambling with investments can be addictive and can turn into a dangerous game that can put you back years, if not decades on your wealth journey if you aren't careful. As a rule of thumb, I refuse to gamble and in turn avoid the temptation of falling into the trap.

## Summary to Wealth Creation

So we have given you a crash course on wealth creation and it looks pretty simple right? Exactly! Wealth creation doesn't need to be rocket science and we go back to our three step formula for simple, sustainable and scalable. The idea of this is to remove all possible overwhelm and give you the ability to take action. Your wealth creation action plan is as follows;

1.  Jump on the book portal at book.wealth-mentor.com.au and review the videos for this section along with downloading the activities and worksheets.

2.  Once you have completed the foundations, you should have a very good idea of your budget surplus and where your surplus is being allocated, either to household debts or leaving some left over for wealth creation.

3.  Get clear on your attitude to risk and volatility, your preference for investing and your goals.

4.  Research some investment options that suit your risk profile, whether that be residential property, direct shares, index funds or other options.

5.  Work out how you will commence your investment strategy and decide on an initial and ongoing investment, where possible looking to contribute at a regular automated frequency using the 'pay yourself first' formula.

6.  Make a time to review your portfolio and decide whether you can afford to increase your regular contribution half yearly.

My personal investment strategy involves my business, residential property and index funds. I contribute to the index funds using an administration platform or 'wrap platform' as this platform allows me to automate my contribution strategy along with manage my tax reporting and minimizes the amount of administration I need to complete to manage my investments and get ready for tax time. This 'set and forget' style allows me to invest in a diversified portfolio across the entire world having a regular monthly direct debit which I increase every quarter. The particular index fund I use is a pre-mixed fund with Vanguard who is the largest manager of passive investments in the world and the fund is called the Vanguard Diversified High Growth Index fund which has averaged 8.34% PA since they started in 2002. I personally like Vanguard as they have a wide variety of funds ranging from pre-mixed funds like this one all the way to country specific funds and specialist funds such as emerging markets for those wanting more risk in their portfolio.

I believe in simplicity as compounding is where the magic is. This allows me to have a well diversified portfolio with a low management fee and allows me to focus on living my life and running my business.

I urge you to find the right solution for you and of course if you want to review your portfolio or get started with investing please don't hesitate to reach out and we can ensure you get the right guidance based on what you want to achieve.

# CHAPTER 8

# Travelling Efficiently: Wealth Management

Some of my best clients who have the greatest potential to achieve financial freedom tend to overlook the process of managing their wealth. As humans, we tend to fall into habits quickly, and if we do something that works well once, we continue to do the same thing until it stops working. We can refer to this as *one-trick-pony syndrome*, and it is important to mix things up to ensure that you are making the most of your money as you progress further on your journey.

I remember a friend of mine pouring his heart out to me when he was having problems with his long-term partner, whom he had been with for over ten years. They had kids together, had built a life together, and for as long as they could remember, had always been by each other's side. As a good friend, I tried my best to understand his situation and offer him some advice from an outsider's perspective.

"We have an amazing life, and I love her to death, but we seem to be drifting apart," he told me as he stared down at the ground.

"Well, what do you think has changed? Can you recall when you started to notice a difference?" I inquired to dig a little deeper.

"Everything is fantastic. The kids are great. We have lots of fun together. But . . . the sex . . ." He went silent.

"What about it?"

"Well . . . there just isn't much of it anymore. I can't even remember the last time we got physical, and I think that's the biggest issue."

So that was the source of the problem. The beginning of this book started with the end of most marriages coming from money issues. Most of the remaining issues in a relationship come from the sex (or lack thereof).

I am not a sex counsellor, but having four sisters and having had several long-term relationships, I know what happens after you have been with someone for a while. Things start to get a little stale, and you need to make an effort to mix things up. As a male, I know a lot of us are guilty of relying on our "go-to moves" a little too often. All of you readers know how things normally go:

1. You meet someone and hit it off with lots of chemistry.

2. The first time is full of passion and excitement as you try to explore and learn what makes the other tick.

3. After a while, you should have learned exactly what your partner likes and how to please him or her.

4. You start to worry less about the excitement and get straight to the point of what you know works.

5. Your signature moves start to lose their charm, and your sessions tend to get shorter and shorter.

6. Soon enough, the excuses start rolling in, and the frequency of sessions decreases.

7. Sex turns into a chore, and it seems harder and harder to break the habit.

Sound familiar? Well, it sure does to me, and it definitely did for my friend. You can't just continue to do the same old tricks and expect to get the same outcome. You need to understand where you are on your journey in life, in your relationship, or in your wealth plan so that you can ensure that you make the right decisions to keep things exciting and moving along.

It is no coincidence that money and relationships share so many similarities, and one of my mentors once told me that how you do anything in life is how you do everything. Think about how you choose to show up in all aspects of your life, whether that be at work, with your partner, with your kids, or with your friends, and see the similarities in how you conduct yourself in all those aspects of your life. If you aren't content with how you show up, and how you show up isn't congruent with who you want to be, then change it! Break out of your habits, get a new job, make new friends, share new experiences with your partner, bust out some new moves in the bedroom, and craft the life that you want to live!

Let's get back on topic and leave the topic of relationships and sex for my next book!

The process of wealth management is about keeping on top of what you have and being able to adapt and adjust your plan to what is going on around you. Much like a relationship, wealth management is about nurturing what you have and continuing to build it into a flourishing tree that provides you with fulfillment and joy. The reason many people overlook the stage of wealth management is that most believe that their wealth will take care of itself and that passive income or growth should come without any involvement from them.

Let's use another example to explain.

You planted a seed for an oak tree in your backyard because you wanted to have a shady place for your kids to play in the future. You know that oak trees take a long time to grow and at a rate of around four metres every ten years, but you are OK with that, as you know that good things take time. In the beginning, you know you need to water the seed, protect it from the elements, and ensure it is given love and attention in order for it to grow. As it grows from a small seed into a bigger sapling, you understand that this is the most vulnerable time.

So, knowing all of this, do you just plant the seed and hope for the best?

Our goal is to help our clients to plant as many seeds as possible and create a way in which they can care for them all in a simple and straightforward manner that gives them the best opportunity to reach their potential. As your wealth trees continue to grow, we need to be considerate of the hurdles that may present themselves and how these hurdles may impact your future planning.

Planting a tree in the wrong place in your backyard can result in cracking concrete, plumbing blockages, or disputes with neighbours. Similarly, it is important that we manage our wealth appropriately by being considerate of things that may come up along the way.

Our wealth management stage should consider the following:

1.  Growing your investments tax effectively.
2.  Keeping on top of your wealth.
3.  Diluting concentrated investment positions.
4.  Creating a wealth pyramid.

Our four stages of wealth management aim to help you maximize your opportunities, create multiple layers to your portfolio, and effectively keep on top of your wealth as it grows and increases in complexity. Additionally, our wealth management process aims to assist you in making the right investment decisions for what you want to achieve and implementing proven accumulation strategies that can reduce risk and maximize returns for the future.

# Keeping on top of Your Wealth

Have you ever thought about why athletes rarely maintain their position as the number one in their field? Whether it be in athletics, combat sports, or formula one racing, the elite champions of the world always seem to fall from grace eventually.

I am an avid fight fan, and I have been watching the UFC since I was a teenager. As a kid growing up, I was a huge fan of Anderson Silva, who was one of the greatest martial artists of all time and who was able to hold his world title for over 2,400 days, with ten consecutive title defences. For most combat sports athletes, this feat is hard to comprehend.

As I watched each of his title defences, I started to see something change in the way he approached his fights. He became more complacent and cockier, and he took more risks. Eventually he was defeated, and everything he had worked hard to create was torn down in the ring in two rounds against his hungry opponent.

Why is this story relevant to wealth management? It is a great example of the importance of having a milestone to work toward as a means to keep working. Let's dive into this further.

Imagine you are an elite athlete and you have dedicated your life to your craft. You haven't made much money yet, but everyone tells you that you have what it takes to be the best. You train every day, you know what you want, and you are prepared to do whatever it takes to become the world champion. You obsess about it daily, visualizing yourself wearing the gold medal, carrying the huge trophy, and standing in front of all your screaming fans.

After five years of hard work, blood, sweat, and tears, your dreams come true. You become the champion of the world, and you achieve all the success you could have ever wanted.

What next?

My old man always said to me "When you get to the top, the only way is down."

You have worked so hard to build your wealth and bring to life some of the things you once thought were just dreams. You are carrying the trophy for your hard work, and the last thing you want is for it all to crumble around you, right? So how do we keep on top of our wealth to make sure it keeps collecting gold medals for us for decades to come? Well, we need to ensure we regularly review and revise our plan along the way.

Imagine that you have all of your wealth in property and you need to get quick access to cash. Do you really want to sell a substantial asset worth hundreds of thousands when you only need a fraction of that? Staying on top of your wealth and keeping a finger on the pulse is a crucial skill, and it requires the right mindset and frame to maintain. As humans, we are easily distracted by our surroundings, and we tend to get lost in the bright lights of our wealth that can lead us into making poor and ill-informed decisions.

I had a client who was very wealthy and quite a sophisticated investor who had pretty much made it by the age of forty. He had a successful multi-national business that generated him more money than he needed. And with his having a portfolio in excess of $15 million, you would expect that he no longer needed to work hard to manage his money.

Wrong.

Over the time we worked together, I was able to observe how he changed. From a hungry entrepreneur wanting to build a substantial business the right way, he transitioned into a gambler chasing the next sexy opportunity that would give him a thrill. Whether funding a private development in Asia or getting into start-up funding syndicates, he was always looking for the next thing to roll the dice on.

Through the course of our relationship, he went from being ready and willing to take advice to being close-minded and unwilling to seek external input as part of his decision-making process. It was as if no one had earned the right to give him advice, and he was happy to follow his gut in making these decisions.

In all due respect, his gut had gotten him this far, right?

After being at the top for so long, much like Anderson Silva, he started to take excessive risks. His calculated and strategic investment decisions turned into blatant speculation, and over the course of eighteen months, he lost almost 50 percent of his net worth. Luckily for him, he still had substantial means and a healthy business to make up for lost ground, but others like him weren't so lucky.

Wealth management is about being humble and constantly reinforcing a single statement to yourself as a means of accountability:

"I will not take any more risk than I need to reach my desired destination."

Our wealth management strategy remains the same regardless of whether you have $100,000 or $100 million. It involves managing our tax, exiting concentrated positions, and building a wealth pyramid. With these three aspects of your wealth management strategy, you can have peace of mind that you are constantly reviewing your wealth and keeping it under wraps in pursuit of your goals.

## Growing Your Investments Tax-Effectively

Tax is a big contributor or detractor when making investment decisions, and once again, this is an often-overlooked part of wealth management. Much like gamblers talk only about their winnings, many investors talk only about their returns before tax and never take the time to do the math of the net return once all the dust has settled.

Here's a quick crash course on tax. Depending on the investment, there are generally two key tax considerations: income and capital growth.

Income is self-explanatory and includes any income stream that is received from an investment, such as rent, dividends, or distributions. In Australia, based on current rules, net income (income minus related costs for holding the investment) is added to your assessable income for the year, and you will pay your marginal tax rate on that income. It is important to also note that some income has already been taxed, particularly when we receive dividends from owning shares that have franking credits, meaning the company already paid tax on the distribution.

An example is that an individual who earns $80,000 per annum would normally pay $19,147 in tax. Assuming the same person had a property that after costs created $5,000 in net income, this individual's tax bill would go up to $20,872, meaning that this person would only receive $3,275 after tax on the property.

By comparison, if the same person had a portfolio of shares that generated $5,000 in dividends already taxed at 30 percent, this person's taxable income would be $18,729 due to having $2,142 in franking credits for the tax-paid dividends. As you can see, not all income is the same.

Capital growth is the amount an investment increases above the price you paid for it. We do not pay tax on capital growth until the asset is sold (or deemed to be sold). And in Australia, we are lucky to have some of the best capital gains discounts in the developed world. The capital gains tax you pay is dependent on how long you owned the asset and is as follows:

**Less than twelve months**—The capital gain (the sale price and sale costs minus the purchase price and purchase costs) is added to assessable income for that year for owners of asset.

**More than twelve months**—The capital gain (the sale price and sale costs minus the purchase price and purchase costs) is discounted by 50 percent, and the remaining 50 percent is added to assessable income for that year for owners of asset.

For example, an individual who earns $80,000 per annum would normally pay $19,147 in tax. That individual bought a property in 2005 for $500,000, including costs such as stamp duty and legal fees, and sold it in 2017 for $1,000,000, including costs such as agent sales commission and legal fees. The capital gain is $500,000, which is discounted by 50 percent, or $250,000, for being owned longer than a year. This $250,000 is added to the individual's assessable income of $80,000 for the year, and the total tax bill would be $128,332, with a tax bill of $109,185 for the property itself. In this instance, the net return is $390,815, or 78% of the original purchase price, which works out to around 6.5 percent per annum over twelve years.

I am sure all of you really dislike tax, and I totally agree. Tax is a pain in the ass. Unfortunately, there are only two certainties in life, death and taxes, so we need to look at tax as being a consequence of making money. When it comes to building wealth, our tax strategy coincides with our bucket strategy, as each bucket will normally have different tax outcomes based on how your assets are owned.

This book is designed to be a first step toward awareness, so I want to give you just enough information so that you can ask the right questions based on your situation. The Australian tax system is extremely complex, and there are countless rules and regulations to consider, so I would recommend anyone who is looking to build wealth tax effectively to get proper tax advice. We will cover this, who you should choose, in more detail later in this book.

As a quick-start guide, I have included some key considerations for all of the main assets you may consider as part of your wealth strategy along with where they normally fit in your bucket strategy. This will help you understand the potential tax considerations that need to be assessed before making a decision.

## Short-Term Bucket—Less than Twelve Months

Cash, bonds, and fixed interest

**Considerations**—Because cash does not appreciate in value or experience growth, the only key consideration is income that will be added to your marginal tax rate. Be mindful of your taxable income and how a return can be eroded after tax. Compare it to inflation to ensure that it is equal to or above inflation or else it will be going backward and losing value.

## Medium-Term Bucket—Twelve Months up to Age Sixty

Shares, managed funds, index funds

**Considerations**—Shares and managed funds can offer some tax benefits for income due to franking credits and due to capital appreciation potential. They can also receive the benefits of capital gains discounting if owned for more than twelve months. Remember, tax is only paid on growth if you ever sell, so for most, the aim is to continue to accumulate.

Direct property

**Considerations**—Residential property in Australia has been a solid asset class that has allowed investors to experience a good balance of income and growth. Net income is determined after costs for holding the property, such as interest on loans, rates, insurance, and management fees, have been deducted. If this number is a negative, you can claim this from your taxable income as a deduction. Positive cash flow in property is what many people aim for, but the rate of return can be considerably lower than with other investments due to the high costs of holding a property. Additionally, capital gains potential can be high, and property can also benefit from capital gains tax discounting if held for more than twelve months.

### Long-Term Bucket—Age Sixty Plus

Superannuation- all assets

**Considerations**—Superannuation is the most tax effective way in Australia to hold investments, as superannuation has several concessional tax rules that allow you to reduce your tax on investment returns. The tax rules are broken into two main sections: preretirement (under age sixty to age sixty-five) and postretirement (ages sixty to sixty-five plus)

Based on the current rules the basic considerations are as follows:

### Preretirement—Under Age Sixty to Age Sixty-Five

**Income**—Taxed at 15 percent

**Capital growth**—Taxed at 15 percent if held less than twelve months and 10 percent if more than twelve months

Postretirement—Ages Sixty to Sixty-Five Plus

**Income**—No tax

**Capital growth**—No tax

Be mindful that the rules have been changed a lot by the government. Currently, if you are between the ages of sixty and sixty-five, you must be fully retired to be able to qualify for the no-tax concessions. Additionally, the government has recently capped this tax-free amount to a maximum of $1.6 million per person. Depending on when you read this book, it is important to seek advice around this because the rules can change anytime.

## Diluting Concentrated Investment Positions

Let's face it—most people first get started in building wealth using a small selection or a single investment. Whether that be our first property purchase or a small parcel of shares we inherited from our grandparents, we tend to start small and work our way up. For most of my clients, we commence building the core of their portfolio using residential property, either as their own home or as an investment property, mainly due to the leverage capabilities available to us in Australia. As we discussed in previous chapters around the power of leverage, even a steady and modest return of 4.5 percent of the total asset can result in a substantial magnification effect on your personal investment, which has resulted in many Australians doing very well with property.

As we know, property is an illiquid asset class, and we can't sell the kitchen sink if we want to go to the Bahamas and sip rum from a coconut. As such, we need to be conscious of how we dilute our investments, which may present risks in our portfolio. For example, many investors use the equity they build in their home or investment properties to get additional cash from the bank against this equity to fund additional property purchases. This is one way of achieving this objective, but this still leads to having all of their money tied in a single asset class.

Our approach to portfolio construction is using a strategy called *core-satellite*, in which we aim to start with our core portfolio, whether that be property, and then look to layer in additional investments over time in order to allow us to build a robust and diversified mix of assets.

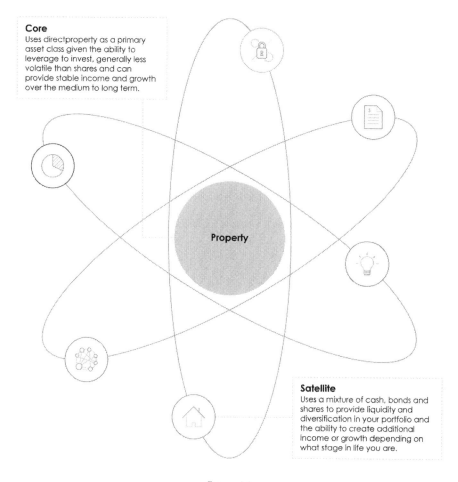

**Core**
Uses directproperty as a primary
asset class given the ability to
leverage to invest, generally less
volatile than shares and can
provide stable income and growth
over the medium to long term.

**Property**

**Satellite**
Uses a mixture of cash, bonds and
shares to provide liquidity and
diversification in your portfolio and
the ability to create additional
income or growth depending on
what stage in life you are.

Figure 14

# Creating a Wealth Pyramid

A wealth pyramid is one of the best ways I can explain how a complete
portfolio should look. It gives us a clear picture of what we should strive
for when building our dream portfolio in pursuit of financial freedom.
Once again, it is about linking each part of your portfolio to a purpose,
much like the bucket strategy, with an aim of having complete clarity of
which asset serves which purpose.

With anything in life, we need to have the right tools for the right job, and each investment has very different characteristics that need to be linked back to you. Imagine for a second you want to go 4x4 driving on the sand dunes. Would you ever consider doing this in a Mini Cooper? You could try, but I expect that you would very quickly become bogged, and someone with a suitable car would have to rescue you.

Our wealth pyramid allows us to break down our complete plan toward financial freedom into three components: the base, middle, and the summit. Each of these areas has a specific purpose in our wealth management plan.

**Base**—Our base is aimed to be the core of our portfolio that we know is tried and true. It should be consistent, and it is aimed to allow us to cover our basic needs and fixed costs from passive income. This includes cash, bonds, blue chip shares, and residential property in affluent areas.

**Middle**—Assuming our base is formed, and our basic needs are met, the middle is aimed to allow us to amplify our lifestyle and is aimed toward growth investments that will allow us to replace our lifestyle expenditure and discretionary spending. Although this part of our portfolio is more volatile, we understand that it will provide us with substantial growth over the long term. This includes high-growth shares, small company stocks, emerging markets, and other high-growth investments.

**Summit**—The summit is considered when our entire lifestyle costs are covered and secure, and this part of our strategy allows us to take some additional risks in pursuit of financial abundance. These investments can be more speculative. But only use a pre-determined level of funds that will not cause your pyramid to come tumbling down if they do not pay off.

This could include investing in private companies, start-ups, development syndicates, or other very high-risk opportunities.

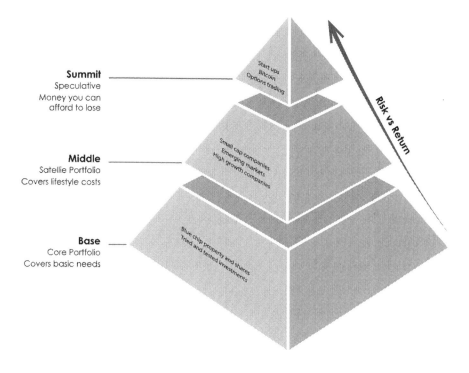

**Summit**
Speculative
Money you can
afford to lose

**Middle**
Satellie Portfolio
Covers lifestyle costs

**Base**
Core Portfolio
Covers basic needs

Start ups
Bitcoin
Options trading

Small cap companies
Emerging markets
High growth companies

Blue chip property and shares
Tried and tested investments

Risk vs Return

Figure 15

The important point of creating a wealth pyramid, along with the bucket strategy, is that this allows you to pay careful consideration to your needs, wants, and desires and look objectively to your portfolio as a solution to these needs, wants, and desires. This allows you to evaluate, either on your own or with an advisor or mentor, whether you need to adjust your portfolio, pursue new opportunities, or reduce your appetite for risk based on what you are working toward.

Throughout my professional career, I always tried to help my father and give him the right advice. As it is with many ethnic fathers, my advice was not always well received, because he always thought he knew better. It seemed as though he would do the exact opposite of the advice I gave him. After a while, I got fed up with trying.

We went through a really tough time financially when he first was diagnosed with cancer, and after separating from his wife at the time, he was really financially up the creek without a paddle. With a substantial mortgage hanging over his head, financial commitments coming out of his ears, and a mountain of bad debts used as a means of survival, he still wouldn't ask me for help.

At this time, he was on the verge of losing his home, and I needed to step in. We were lucky because the property had gone up quite significantly in value, and the equity in the property was enough to get him out of hot water. For obvious reasons, the bank wouldn't lend him any more money. After all, how was he going to pay for it?

"Dad, you really need help to get out of this situation. Let me do something so we can sort this all out." I pleaded to him, hoping he would let me in.

"There's nothing you can do, Jack. This is my problem, so it shouldn't have to become your burden." He replied without a second's thought.

"Well, where are you going to live? You know they are going to force you to sell the house, and we will end up with nothing. Is that what you really want?"

I hit a heart string. My dad's house was always his castle, and I knew he didn't want to be forced to leave. We had so many memories there, and this place was a symbol of his hard work and dedication in an attempt to get ahead in life.

There was a silence. I didn't dare speak a word.

"So, what can we do about this?" he asked abruptly as he tried to overcome his own defences.

"Our only option is for me to go on the title for 1 percent, and that will allow me to use my income to service the loan we need to fix these things up. We can pay out your ex-wife, consolidate all of your debts, and we can work together to tackle the mortgage."

He pondered for a moment.

"Are you sure you are OK with this?" he asked me, noticeably embarrassed for having to drag me into his mess.

"Of course, Dad. This is our home, and we'll do what it takes."

We saved the house, paid out his ex-wife, consolidated all of his debts, and kept working together to keep on top of the repayments. During this time, the property market was going gangbusters, and our modest apartment more than doubled in value. Great news, right?

Dad was sixty-five now, and after a lifetime of hard work, it was time to start winding down. With all of his wealth tied up in his home, I suggested that he look to sell and move out of Sydney to where he could get a nice piece of land with no mortgage and live a basic life that was comfortable for him and his new partner. We had the property on the market for twelve months, and after countless offers, negotiations, and lots of back and forth, he wouldn't accept any offers.

"I won't sell unless I get $1,000,000. I am going to get it. I know I will," he said confidently to the real estate agent every time someone would come with an offer.

"But Mario, there are comparable properties selling in the market for $800,000 to $850,000. There is no way anyone will pay what you are asking," replied the agent, trying to reason with him.

"I want what I want. If they don't want to pay, I don't want to sell."

After seven years of remission, my father was diagnosed with cancer again. This time it was pretty serious, and it escalated very quickly. With this new sense of urgency, we continued to try to sell the property with no success, and as of writing this book, the property is still yet to be sold. The offers received were substantially lower than previous offers, and a window of opportunity was clearly missed.

So, what is the moral of this story, and what does it have to do with the wealth pyramid?

Well, it highlights the need for you to have context for your investment-making decisions. Having a point of reference in your plan can ultimately assist you in making the right decisions at the right time. We will never get it 100 percent perfect. And in hindsight, if he would have sold the property and purchased another one, that may not have changed a thing. What could have changed was the impact of assessing the cost-benefit of his decision-making process.

- What was the cost of twelve months of time of open home inspections, negotiations with buyers, drafting of legal contracts, and so on?

- What was the lost opportunity for not selling the property at the peak of the market when the highest price was demanded?

The point of this is, don't pursue a reckless mindset of complete abundance when it impedes your ability to achieve your basic needs, wants, and desires.

## Summary To Wealth Management

Wealth management is all about having the right layer to your portfolio to allow you to work towards your three stages of passive income; covering basic needs, lifestyle costs and cream on top. Your wealth management action plan is as follows;

1. Jump on the book portal at book.wealth-mentor.com.au and review the videos for this section along with downloading the activities and worksheets.

2. You need to work out how much you need at each stage of your wealth pyramid to achieve each stage.

3. Review this against your current portfolio which will help you decide where you should continue to allocate your surplus or reinvest your earnings.

4. Consider utilizing a wealth management dashboard such as MyProsperity that will help you keep track of all of your finances in a single place.

5. Ensure you have structured your bucket strategy based on your stage of life.

6. If needed, ensure you are getting the right guidance on how you are best to manage your wealth to keep on track for your goals.

Once again, having a simple approach to wealth management takes the complexity around how you continue to scale your wealth in pursuit of your destination. Wealth management is about efficiency and reevaluating how you approach decisions depending on what outcome you are trying to achieve so take some time to compare this against how you currently manage your wealth and see how it compares.

I know from first hand experience, wealth management can become a job in itself if not setup correctly so if you are having troubles here please reach out.

CHAPTER 9

# What Happens When You Get There: Wealth Legacy

Legacy is one of the most-often-overlooked parts of wealth planning, yet almost all of the clients I have worked with have some aspiration to give back in some way, either to those around them or to something they are passionate about.

This stage of our plan is a process of self-actualization. It also is a point at which we have achieved our own ambitions or wishes for have personal gain and are in a comfortable position to start giving back to others. This can be one of the most enjoyable parts of planning, as it allows us to play an active role in having a significant impact in the world.

Our legacy can be broken up into a number of segments:

1. Future Generation Planning.

2. Charity & Philanthropy.

3. Estate Planning.

It is a common misconception that legacy is all about when we are no longer here. In my experience, it is becoming more commonplace that people are planning for their legacy in their lifetimes so that they can enjoy the fulfillment of seeing the impact their contributions can make to their various beneficiaries. With this being said, it is important to think about your legacy as you progress along your journey to ensure that you are clear on what you want to see happen if the worst were to happen.

Let's get the warm and fuzzy stuff out of the way first before we reverse the hearse and talk about the things we would prefer not to talk about.

# Future Generation Planning

In Sydney, on the Northern Beaches, it is pretty commonplace for parents to want to send their kids to private school. Whether the parents want to send them to the same school that they went to or whether they have another aspiration, that doesn't change the fact that it is bloody expensive!

Although there are many options available, the cheapest semi-private options range from around $5,000 per annum plus extras all the way to over $30,000 per annum for full private. If a child goes to private school for all of his or her secondary schooling, that can total over $200,000. Multiply that by multiple kids, and you have some sleepless nights ahead (or a need for careful planning).

Furthermore, we are seeing that most Australians are concerned about how their kids will get into the property market, given the huge growth we have experienced over the last decade. Many parents want to be able to help their kids get a foot in the door of the property market and ensure that they don't have to battle as hard as they did to be a homeowner.

As with anything in life, the sooner you start, the easier the journey, and we need to understand the variables at play before we dive in feet first. When considering your future generation plan, ask yourself the following:

1.  What are you trying to achieve? (Saving for school fees, deposit, first car, etc.)

2.  How much in total does it cost today? ($180,000 for school; $80,000 for deposit; $30,000 for car)

3.  When do you need the money available? (Ten years, fifteen years, twenty years)

With these three simple questions, we can start working toward what the future value needs to be after inflation has been factored in, and we can work out how much we need to put away to achieve the goal.

If you want to get some help with working through this and ensuring you consider how future generation planning might affect your overall plan, get in touch with us so we can help you.

Once we define our target number, how much we want to contribute, and how long we have to wait, we then need to work out what we are going to do with the money. There are a few considerations here, and I will run through three options that my clients typically use, depending on their situation.

## Pay Extra Money into Home Loan and Redraw When Needed

If you are like many people and you have a significant mortgage still outstanding, then you might be inclined to put every extra dollar you can into trying to pay it off as quickly as possible. I personally have no issue with this. As outlined earlier in this book, paying off your home loan is a risk-free return on your money due to the interest saved as a result of your contribution, but there are some key drawbacks you need to carefully consider.

In my experience, keeping all of your money in one big pot doesn't give you much transparency around what money is meant for what. Especially if you are making extra contributions month after month for years, it can get pretty difficult to track which money carries which purpose. Having said that, some banks do offer a function called a *multiple offset account*, which lets you have small buckets of money for a specific purpose while having all of those pots linked to your mortgage and reducing the interest paid. This can be a great strategy, but it's not ideal for those who want to have their savings out of reach.

This solution is best if you have short-term savings goals or don't want to worry about the volatility or tax consequences of your investments. If you believe you might need extra transparency around your savings or else you might give in to temptation having the money sitting there in your online banking, this option might not be for you.

## Setting Up an Investment Account to Purchase Shares or Managed Funds

When we are building wealth for the long term, it is always good to consider putting money into growth assets given their historical performance compared with other alternatives. Especially when our goals are for over a decade of time, investing in shares can provide us with both income and growth in pursuit of the end goal.

When buying shares or managed funds, we need to consider a number of aspects that relate to volatility and taxation. Volatility is an unknown variable with any growth investment, and we need to be able to wait it out in order to reap the rewards of our investment. With this volatility in mind, it is important to consider the timeframe you have available. And as you approach the goal, it is important to reconsider your risk profile to ensure that last-minute volatility doesn't impact your ability to fulfil your plans. Additionally, we need to be mindful that investing in assets that grow in value will incur tax, so it is important to get advice on this from a tax professional when it comes time to sell.

This solution is best if you have a long time before you achieve the goal, you want the flexibility to cash in the funds, or if you or your partner are not working or producing income- you can negate some or all of the tax issues by having the assets in his or her name. Don't consider this if you can't stand volatility or if you have short-term goals of less than five years.

## Investment Bonds

Investment bonds are an underused investment structure that work really well for long-term planning. Much like managed funds or shares, an investment bond does the same but within a special tax structure that comes with its own rules and regulations. In summary, an investment bond allows the following:

- You contribute money into the investment from your after-tax income.

- The money is invested into an investment option you select ranging from low risk to high risk.

- Any earnings made on the investment get taxed at a flat rate of 30 percent.

- No further tax is paid by you personally.

- If you hold the investment for more than ten years, it becomes tax-free with no capital gains to be paid.

Considering that in some instances, capital gains tax can be 25 percent of your growth earnings, investment bonds can be a significant difference in the net outcome of your investment. It is important to note that investment bonds do come with some restrictions.

- You can only contribute 125 percent of what you put in the year before (e.g., $1000 this year means $1,250 maximum next year).

- If you miss a year of contributions, you cannot contribute again, or you restart the ten-year rule.

- You can access money at any time, but drawing money out within the ten years may result in your paying some additional tax (which would be a comparable outcome to the previous option of shares or managed funds held directly).

The key to investment bonds is getting your ongoing contributions right up front. If you need to save $200,000, then it is unlikely that starting with $50 per month will get you there in ten years. Given the 125 percent rule, it is important you do your math correctly. This structure works great for those who want money out of sight and working behind the scenes with some lucrative tax benefits. But once again, it is a little more complex and does come with some restrictions that need careful planning.

If you want to explore any of these options as part of your future generation planning, feel free to reach out to us to discuss further.

## Charity and Philanthropy

Most of us at some time have wanted to give back to a cause, whether that be helping out your family, donating to charity, or giving back to the less fortunate. When we think of philanthropy, we immediately think of the super wealthy like Bill Gates or Angelina Jolie who seem to give endlessly to those in need. The truth is, we don't need to be super wealthy to give back to a cause we believe in.

Once again, this comes down to allocation of surplus.

I know I must sound like a broken record, but this is a really important point. Wealth management is quite simple if we understand how much we have available to allocate toward our goals. For the purposes of this exercise, let's assume that you know you are on track for your other goals and that you have a pre-defined amount you want to contribute toward the greater good.

In my experience, most people approach philanthropy the wrong way. Bold statement? I agree.

But Jackson, how can anyone possibly approach charity the wrong way?

Let me take a moment to explain. Charity is a complex beast, and many overlook the details of how much of their donation actually reaches their intended destination. Have you given much thought to the costs of running the charity, putting donation collectors on the streets, and putting ads on television? All of these things are expensive and, in turn, erode the actual amount sent to the cause. Of course, all businesses cost money to run, and you would expect that there would be very few charities that send 100 percent of your contribution to the people in need. But how much on average do they spend on keeping the machine running?

In a recent study by **CHOICE**, it was found that in many cases, Australian charities are spending more than 83 percent of their donations to keep the doors open! There have also been instances wherein some charities have spent 110 percent of their donations, which is a scary thought. With the bulk of your contribution potentially going to administration fees, sales commissions, and other costs, you might ask yourself why you should even bother. The key to having success in your charity initiatives is having a clear goal and doing your due diligence.

Our five-step process to charitable giving is as follows:

1. Clearly define your values.

2. Have a mission you want to achieve.

3. Know how much you want to contribute (either time or money).

4. Identify your options.

5. Do your research.

As with any investment, we need to work toward what we aim to achieve so that we can make the right decisions in pursuit of the goal. We have created a simple checklist to help you when doing your research to ensure that you find the right charity that aligns with your values:

**Charity Checklist:**

- If you're donating to an overseas aid organization, check that it's a member of the Australian Council for International Development (ACFID), which will give you some certainty around how it is supervised and regulated.

- For domestic charities and commercial fundraisers, ask if they're a member of the Fundraising Institute of Australia and are registered with the Australian Charities and Not-for-profits Commission.

- Do your own research to find out the running costs and administration expenses for the charity you want to contribute to so that you can see how much actually goes to the cause. Additionally, check for independent research reports on your charity, which can save you some of the heavy lifting.

For most of us, donating money or time to a charity is the simplest way to make a difference. For those of you who want to take things to the next level, due to having either an abundance of time or resources to contribute, you may want to consider starting your own charitable foundation. Given the complexity of this, we won't go into too much detail in this book. But if you want to discuss how you can pursue a more active role in philanthropy, please get in touch with us so that we can help you navigate the tips and traps.

At The Wealth Mentor and as part of Aureus Financial, we aim to revolutionize the way that everyday people get access to wealth education. As such, we donate 10 percent of all profits to improving financial literacy in Australia. Our aim is to establish a charitable foundation that will allow us to play an active role in the integration of practical financial skills in the educational system from K–12.

We will be providing updates around the progress of our charitable program throughout 2018 so ensure you keep an eye on our Facebook Group for more information.

# Estate Planning

But Jackson, you already covered this earlier in your book. *Yes,* I know! For years I have been trying to convince my clients to invest the time into considering their estate plan, and it is something we always put on the list of things to do but tend to never get around to resolving. Given the grim subject of death, most of us don't want to come to terms with the potential risks associated with not having a proper estate plan, and we prefer to forget about it. This is why I want to reiterate the importance of estate planning and ensure that you get it done ASAP.

For us advisers, there is never an easy time to talk about these things with our clients, but this is one of those things that can carry catastrophic consequences if not dealt with properly, with the right advice. This topic is aimed to help you understand the risks, come to terms with what you need to address, and get it done once and for all.

### What is Estate Planning?

Estate planning is taking the time to carefully consider what you want to see happen to your assets and how you want them dealt with in the event of your passing. Most people generally understand this as having a valid will in place that will list all of your wishes to be dealt with in your absence. Unfortunately, this is not always the case, and there are some considerable complexities that can arise as a result of not having the appropriate measures in place.

## Why is It Important?

Having a proper estate plan ensures that you are able to carefully document your wishes, provide guidance to your estate around how you wish for your assets to be distributed, and document any other specific bequests you may have. This is a process of your being able to play an active role in how you are remembered and, in turn, the experience your family has in result of your passing.

In the event that you pass away without a valid will, this is referred to as "intestate," which means that the courts will be responsible for determining how your assets will be distributed. The potential implications of this may include the following:

- Your assets being distributed to individuals whom you may have wished to exclude from your estate
- Excessive costs to your beneficiaries if they wish to contest the decisions made by the court
- Additional tax implications for your beneficiaries that may have otherwise been avoided

## Key Things to Consider

- Have a professionally written will with backups for your executor, trustees, and beneficiaries.

There is a huge difference between getting a will kit from the post office and having a professional estate specialist write your documents for you. Remember that you are not going to be around to explain the context of your wishes, so if there is any ambiguity in your statements, they can be misinterpreted and lead to lengthy and costly legal battles. Also, it is extremely important that you appoint a primary preference and two backups for the roles of your estate to ensure that if one is not in a position to take on the responsibility, the decision does not fall on the courts, who can be ruthless in their decision making.

- Implement an Enduring Power of Attorney/Enduring Guardianship for medical and financial decisions

Passing away is not always the only outcome of a sickness or accident. As such, it is worthwhile to consider who you wish to be able to make these important financial decisions on your behalf if you were to lose capacity. This is especially important if you have a business, property assets, or other complexities in your financial situation so that you have someone to project manage this in your absence. Additionally, an enduring guardianship appoints a person to make medical decisions on your behalf. This can allow you to provide him or her with direction on how to deal with certain sensitive topics so that he or she doesn't need to feel the pressure to make the right decisions on his or her own.

- Establish guardianship provisions for your dependent children

If you and your partner were to pass away, it is important who you would like the courts to consider as guardians for your children until they are old enough to care for themselves. Given that this is a substantial responsibility, it takes careful consideration and likely a serious conversation to ensure that who you appoint is prepared for this event if it were to happen. It is also important to consider how your estate is able to provide the guardians with the means to care for your dependent children.

- Establish a Testamentary Discretional Trust

This can be one of the most important parts of your estate and can provide your beneficiaries with significant tax and asset protection benefits. We will explain how this works.

## What is a Testamentary Discretional Trust?

A Testamentary Discretionary Trust (TDT) is a trust established in someone's will. It comes into existence only when the person dies. A Lineal Descendant TDT is a trust established in someone's will for the benefit of that person's lineal descendants.

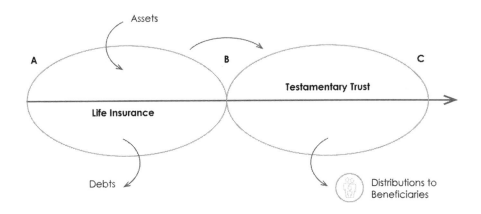

Figure 16

Let's assume that someone dies at point A.

The executor's job involves finding all the assets, paying out any debts, and, usually at point B, distributing what's left to the beneficiaries.

If there is a TDT, part or all of what's left remains in the estate and is distributed later—at any time between point B and point C, depending on the terms of the will. Point C can generally be up to eighty years from point A.

A will can establish more than one TDT.

## Who Controls the Assets?

Whoever is named in the will as trustee controls the TDT's assets. Like any trust, a TDT can be as flexible or as fixed as desired. The trustee can be given full discretion or no discretion as to who should receive income and capital from the TDT and when they should receive it.

The trustee is often the same person who was appointed as executor and can also be a beneficiary. For example, a parent can establish a TDT for each child's inheritance. Each adult child can be the trustee of his or her own trust and may also be an executor.

## Minor Dependents Tax—How Can You Minimize the Cost to Your Estate?

A fact that most people overlook is that minor children may not be able to manage the estate assets themselves, but the beneficial ownership of those assets is still in their names in the event of your leaving an inheritance to them. What this means is that there is a potential for significant tax implications for any income earned. The tax rates for minors are as follows:

Table 3

| Eligible Income | Resident Prescriped Tax Rate Applicable |
| --- | --- |
| $0 - $416 | nil |
| $416 - $1,307 | 66% for amount in excess of $416 |
| $1,308+ | 47% on the entire amount |

So, let's assume you have an insurance policy that pays out $500,000 to your child who is ten years old. This money is invested and earns a marginal rate of 5 percent, which means that the interest earned is $25,000. Based on the above tax rates (see table 3), the total tax liability would be $11,723, or close to 47 percent of the total income earned.

How can a TDT help with this?

Rather than all of the deceased's assets being distributed by the executor upon death, some or all of the assets remain in trust for the benefit of a specific group of beneficiaries named in the will.

Trust income distributed to children, of any age, will be taxed at adult rates rather than the penalty rates that normally apply to minors' unearned income from a standard (non-will-created) trust.

The trustee can have full discretion as to who receives trust income and capital, or restrictions can be provided.

So, based on the same above scenario, if the child receives $25,000 of income from assets within the TDT, the child could receive $18,200 tax-free.

## What Should You Do to Get Advice about These Items?

We advocate for our clients to have their documents created using an estate planning specialist and ensure that they get appropriate advice. As part of our service offering to our clients, we have an estate planning facilitation and complimentary review service if you have existing documents that you want checked.

We have included lots of supporting information in both the foundations and legacy section of the member portal at book.wealth-mentor.com.au to help guide you around this. If you want to discuss this, please get in touch with us via our website, and we can help you sort out all of your estate and legacy needs.

# ACT 3
## TAKING ACTION

# CHAPTER 10

# Creating Your Own Roadmap: The Lifetime Financial Plan

We are getting to the pointy end of this book, and it is now time to map out your plan for what needs to happen next. As you have noticed throughout this book, we have three common themes that will drive all of your future planning moving forward: where are you now, what do you want, and how do you plan to get there? Being considerate of the complexities of life, we need to have a way to keep on top of our plan so that we can use it as a point of reference as we progress and adjust and modify it as we pursue our goals.

Our wealth journey creates a simple point of reference when it comes to thinking about what it is you want in life, by when you want it, and what you will need in order to get there. One of my favourite quotes of all time is "The difference between a dream and a goal is a plan." We want this to be true for you as well.

As a kid I was a serial procrastinator, and I was always a dreamer. It was something I learned from my parents, and looking back, I never had role models in my life who were able to finish the projects they set out in pursuit of. They always set out with the best intentions, but it seemed that time after time, their dreams were crushed in front of their eyes.

I vividly remember that when I was in primary school, my mother had an aspiration to start a second-hand clothing store. She was always passionate about clothing and had previously owned a similar store before I was born, and it was always her dream to open another one and try again.

In our local area of Sutherland, a suburb in southern Sydney, there was a thrift shop that mum always would visit, and it just so happened to come up for sale. My mum was never well-off financially. She managed to scrape together just enough money to buy the business and jumped straight into running her own shop. She loved the freedom of being her own boss. but she never had a plan. She had no real experience in running a business. She didn't know how to do basic business functions such as bookkeeping, saving enough for taxes, budgeting and managing cash flow, or marketing. Her pursuit was driven by pure passion, and in many cases, passion just isn't enough.

I spent a lot of time at the shop, either after school or on the weekend, and I continued to see Mum's passion quickly overcome by stress and responsibility until the burden became too much to bear. As a business owner, or as anyone looking to jump into a plan, you need to either have enough means to buffer your own mistakes as you learn or be willing to be mentored by someone who has made the mistakes already and is willing to teach you how to avoid them yourself. As we all know, mistakes and learning can be costly. In most cases, we have only a finite capacity to make these mistakes before we need to chuck in the towel.

Unfortunately for Mum, she had very limited means to make mistakes. She was reliant on her business income to keep the wheels turning. She also took out some loans with family members and friends to keep her head above water. The lack of a plan meant she was navigating completely unchartered territory. It was no longer a strategic pursuit—it was a game of chance.

As I started to see the unopened bills pile up on the kitchen bench, I could sense something was wrong, even as a small child. Soon thereafter, Mum chose to close down the shop in an admission of defeat. Once again, all of her hard work and dedication seemed to not be enough to set her on the path for success.

Through these tough experiences that I observed my parents go through, I really learned a lot that has made me become a better coach and mentor for my clients. These experiences showed me the necessity to have a well-thought-out plan, be able to identify and work to our strengths, be honest and protect against our weaknesses, and be willing to ask for help from those who have been there before and are able to guide us through the terrain with less pain, in less time, and, in many cases, for less money.

To understand these variables, we first need to map out our wealth journey, whether that be in pursuit of our business ambitions or for personal financial freedom, so that we can work out what needs to be done and who needs to be involved to get us where we want to go. Our wealth journey process looks as follows:

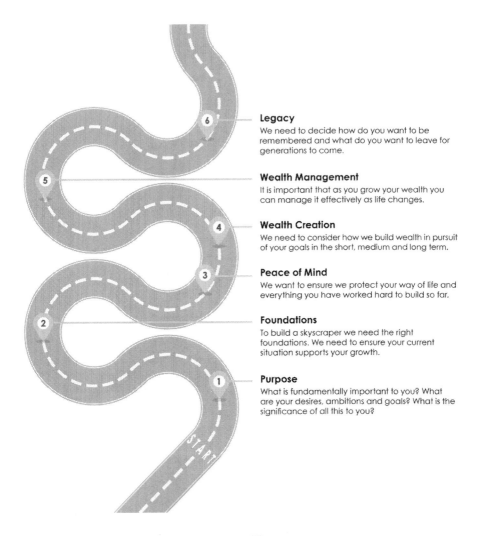

**Legacy**
We need to decide how do you want to be remembered and what do you want to leave for generations to come.

**Wealth Management**
It is important that as you grow your wealth you can manage it effectively as life changes.

**Wealth Creation**
We need to consider how we build wealth in pursuit of your goals in the short, medium and long term.

**Peace of Mind**
We want to ensure we protect your way of life and everything you have worked hard to build so far.

**Foundations**
To build a skyscraper we need the right foundations. We need to ensure your current situation supports your growth.

**Purpose**
What is fundamentally important to you? What are your desires, ambitions and goals? What is the significance of all this to you?

Figure 17

Creating a well-thought-out wealth journey is a process, and we want to ensure you have the right tools to hit the ground running and take action. The last thing we want is for you to lose momentum because you don't know what you should do next when you are mapping out your plan. Our simple action plan is as follows:

1. Go to our member portal at book.wealth-mentor.com.au and download the framework for taking action

2. Complete the "What Are You Working Towards?" exercise, and ask yourself the three questions.

3. Review your foundations and complete the foundations to financial freedom activities

4. Go through your goals and priorities and define what you need for your plan.

5. Work with your accountability partner or reach out to the community to share what you plan to achieve, get it out into the world and use this as a way to hold you accountable to taking action.

6. If you need help navigating the complexities of your situation or if you get stuck please reach out to us

Remember, your plan should be simple, sustainable, and scalable. And where possible, you need to implement the right safety nets to hold yourself accountable to what you plan to do. Far too often, we set out with the best intentions only to watch the candle of motivation flicker and blow out as we fall back into our old habits. This is why having an accountability partner or someone who can help you on the journey is so important, as this increases the probability of getting where you want to go.

From my experience, most people tend to start planning for their wealth goals at two times: (1) when something comes up that they really want or that shocks them into taking action (wanting to buy a home, becoming pregnant, getting divorced, etc.) or (2) after New Year's. How many times have you made a financial New Year's resolution only to fall off the wagon shortly after you set out in pursuit of your goals? We are creatures of habit, and the unfortunate reality is that we have deeply ingrained our bad habits, which are constant hurdles that we need to overcome.

It is time for you to make a decision. Your success in pursuit of your plan will depend on it. Are you ready and committed to do what it takes to achieve your goals? Are you ready to identify the hurdles that may come up along the way? And are you ready to tackle them head on and make new habits that will lead you closer to a life of prosperity and abundance?

As you set out to craft your master plan, I want you to tell yourself the following:

1. I will play an active role in improving my outlook for the future.

2. I will not accept that my reality will remain the same.

3. I know I will make mistakes, but making mistakes in pursuit of my goals is how I will grow.

4. I will make the time I need to create, review, and revise my plan based on what I want.

5. I will ask for help and support when I know I need it.

6. I will share my goals and experience with those around me because they will help me stick to the path.

7. I will do what it takes to reach my desired destination.

I want you to write these affirmations down somewhere and make time to review them regularly with the action items listed above. Remember, future planning is a fluid process, and what you want will always change and evolve. It is important that you constantly keep your goals and desires in mind so that you can ensure you are always playing an active role in pursuit of them.

What happens next is entirely up to you. And I know that with enough time and effort, you will be able to better your position, set yourself on the right path, and achieve what you are looking for.

As Confucius once said "The best time to plant a tree was ten years ago. The second-best time is today." Now it's time to start planning, pick up your shovel, and start planting those seeds so that you can watch them grow and prosper.

CHAPTER 11

# Your Financial Co-pilot: Picking The Right Guide

I have spent the last ten years coaching and mentoring my clients to achieve financial freedom. Over that time, I have had the pleasure of helping change thousands of lives, assisting in accumulating over $1 billion in wealth, and positioning myself as a thought leader in the industry to act as a catalyst for change across the country. Unfortunately, I have also witnessed the dark side of the wealth industry, and I have seen far too many clients who have received bad advice or lost their entire life savings due to dodgy investments.

Although our industry is getting better, with improved government regulation and supervision, there are always bad apples that avoid detection. My mission is to give you the tools and insight you need to choose the right guide to support your journey and filter out those who do not have the necessary skills or expertise to help you get where you need to go.

## When Should I Choose to Look For a Guide?

Some of us have the necessary skills required to do everything needed to work toward a life of financial freedom and abundance without any help at all. These people tend to have a high level of internal accountability, have a good understanding of money and finance, and have completed extensive research in all things wealth to be able to make informed and educated decisions for themselves. These individuals are happy to find solutions to their problems on a transactional basis and will bring people in to help them only on a case-by-case basis.

For everyone else, there is such a steep learning curve, and there are plenty of mistakes to be made along the way to achieve this point. It is often unrealistic to think that you will ever learn more than an experienced professional. For example, if your car blew a head gasket, would you take it to the mechanic to fix, or would you try to do it yourself? If you were a mechanic or engineer, you might be able to, but it also comes down to the value of your time.

You will generally look for a guide if the following applies to you:

- You lack the knowledge or experience to have certainty regarding getting to where you need to go.

- You need someone to hold you accountable to the journey and ensure that you take the necessary steps along the way.

- You are time-poor, and you cannot afford to invest your time to do what it takes to reach your goals.

## What Do I Look For in a Guide?

A guide is a trusted partner and mentor that should be employed to help you achieve certain desired outcomes. You first need to get clear on what you want, and then you can search out the right guide to help you. Guides should have the following:

- A clear value proposition of what they do and how they do it

- A proven track record of experience in the areas you need assistance with

- Access to resources to deliver on their promise

- Ability to provide proof of their experience through accreditations and testimonials

For example, if you are looking for a tax expert, you want someone who is accredited as a tax adviser, who has worked in that field for at least five years, and who is able to showcase how he or she can help along with examples of how he or she has helped others with similar problems.

Be careful when working with generalists who do everything. It is often the case that a jack of all trades is a master of none.

## How Do I Work with a Guide?

Good guides will have a clear methodology of how they work with their clients, whether that be high touch with regular monthly meetings or ad hoc services as you need them. Every guide is different, and they provide services in all shapes and sizes. When choosing a guide and deciding how you work with him or her, you should consider the following:

- Guides should clearly articulate what they aim to provide to you, how often they plan to meet with you, and the costs of their services.

- Guides should also be able to provide you with a flexible package that can be adjusted and tailored to your needs so that you only pay for what you need.

- Guides should be able to clearly articulate how they add value to you, what to expect, and what they expect from you.

- There should be no lock-in period or fixed commitments for you to continue with the guide's services if you no longer want or need them.

- A good guide should provide you with a clear framework of how you will work together and ensure that you are given the right structure and support to guide you on your journey.

## What Should I Pay for a Guide's Services?

This is a tough question, and it ultimately depends on what your guide is doing for you. What you pay should be linked back to the value that is delivered and the outcomes that can be provided to you. It is important to note that a good guide will provide you with both tangible and intangible value that can sometimes be hard to quantify. But guides should be able to illustrate all of the outcomes they provide and how that benefits you. This will allow you to make an informed decision. When considering costs, you should

- consider what improvements you are able to achieve as a result of the quoted fee;

- consider the cost of your time if you tried to achieve the outcomes yourself;

- put a price on the intangible benefits provided to you, such as peace of mind or accountability;

- ensure you understand the cost structure and what you are getting in return;

- understand if your guide receives any commissions or whether any conflicts of interest exist;

- ensure any fees are flat dollar amounts and not a percentage of your wealth; and

- understand if your guide offers any guarantees for his or her work or services to confirm if he or she has skin in the game.

Fees is an often-controversial subject, as fees ultimately depend on what value you place on your goals and objectives. A good guide should be able to articulate the return on investment and what value he or she can provide. A good guide should give you a simple and easy-to-understand fee structure and give you some kind of guarantee that they can deliver on promises.

## What Are the Warning Signs of the Wrong Guide?

This can be a difficult question, and often you need to trust your gut instincts. I have seen bad advice in all shapes and sizes, and more often than not, there are alarm bells that signal something is not quite right. You should be looking for the following signs:

- Your guide is not willing to back up his or her advice with formal written advice.

- Your guide is receiving kickbacks from third-party providers, such as property developers, without being able to justify his or her recommendations.

- Your guide's advice is not supported by appropriate research, track history, or evidence of how it applies to your situation.

- Your guide's recommendations are cookie cutter and generic with no link back to your goals or aspirations.

- Your guide has not been considerate of your attitude to risk, your investment timeline, or your previous experience with investing.

- Your guide is unable to provide references, testimonials, or details of his or her experience, education, or capacity to advise you on what you need.

In summary, you need to be able to ask the right questions and ensure that you complete the necessary due diligence before diving in feetfirst. If it sounds too good to be true, it usually is. And don't be afraid to ask for justification or alternatives based on what you are recommended, because this allows you to make informed and educated decisions.

The right guide should be impartial, should be able to minimize conflicts of interests, and should be working with your best interests at the forefront of his or her mind. Guides should be fighting in your corner and should be able to clearly illustrate what they do, how they do it and what you should expect from working with them. Don't feel pressured to make a knee-jerk decision, and take your time to research your options before you sign anything. We have also included a checklist to help you ask the right questions when you look for a guide on our member portal at book.wealth-mentor.com.au

Remember, some of the worst decisions can come when you don't take enough time to consider what else might be available. This is your future, so you should feel comfortable with how you work toward it and who you choose to guide you there.

My business, Aureus Financial, and its related companies aim to provide a revolutionary approach to wealth coaching and strategic advice by tailoring to everyone's unique situation. Over my career, I have seen the difference quality advice can make. Being able to have access to quality education and mentorship can make all the difference as both an individual and a business owner. Aureus Financial aims to shift the dynamic of most traditional advice relationships by putting you at the centre of everything and empowering you to play an active role in working toward financial freedom while having access to an expert team to support your journey.

Our offering ranges from DIY e-learning courses to help you fill the gaps in your knowledge and work out your plan at an attainable price all the way to full bespoke advice and access to our "Wealth Hub," which is a team of experts who give you access to everything you will ever need, including financial advice, coaching, lending, investment advice, accounting, tax help, and everything in between.

We offer everyone access to a complimentary discovery meeting where we will start mapping out your wealth journey and showing you what you can be doing to make your goals and dreams a reality. We offer every client we engage with a money-back guarantee, so you have 100 percent certainty that we are working for you and with you to get you to where you want to go in life.

If you want to discuss your plan or
even want to get a second opinion,
don't hesitate to reach out and book a time at

www.aureusfinancial.com.au

# Conclusion

As I come close to completing this book, I have taken some time to reflect on my own journey, which I have tried to share with you openly and honestly. As a twenty-eight-year-old, I have endured some tough times, and there have been many instances in which I could have given up and taken the easy route. Through this experience I have learned that the best things in life never come easy, and through our hardest battles come the most satisfying victories.

In my experience, there is something to learn from every battle in life, and I have found strength in being confident enough to share my stories with anyone. My father once told me that unless we learn from our history, we risk repeating it. And once again, his wise words have left a long-lasting impact on me and how I live my life. I want you to come to terms with your experience and share your battles, both good and bad, with those around you to learn from. Failure is nothing to be ashamed of. It is something to be proud of because it stands as proof that you tried.

There is one thing for sure: in pursuit of improvement, there will always be failure. We will always encounter times where we will fall flat on our faces without a second's notice. We often learn to avoid these experiences, shy away from failure, and play it safe. It is this fear of failure that prevents us from growing. Do you want to be that person who looks back on your life in regret of all the things you never tried, the risks you never took, and the opportunities that you never explored?

I know that on my father's deathbed, he recognized that he had lived a life that was full. He experienced the world, he followed his heart, he loved and lost, and he raised a son that admired him more than he would ever know. He raised me in such a way as to not be afraid of the fall, to be able to get back up, dust myself off, and try again for however long it would take. He raised me to fail fast, to rise up to my potential, and to look at ways to change the world and those around me each and every day.

I want to have the privilege one day for my son or daughter to write about my legacy and the lessons they learned from me. I hope that I have the honour of reading their words and being able to watch as they embark on their own journey, pursue their own destination, and chase their purpose until their last days. In the meantime, I want you to do this for yourself and be the catalyst for change for generations to come for all of those you love.

I want you to break the cycle and inspire change. Work to your strengths and embrace your weaknesses. Empower others. And in turn, empower yourself and work toward what you really want in life, not just what society pressures you to do. Power on in spite of adversity, find strength in defeat, be humbled by success, and try your best to make a difference and share your experience.

Remember, you deserve to be successful based on what you define to be success. I wish you the best of luck, and I believe in you.

Signed,

# Jackson Millan- The Wealth Mentor